Becky Freeman

HARVEST HOUSE PUBLISHERS
Eugene, Oregon 97402

Published in association with the literary agency of Alive Communication, Inc., 7680 Goddard St., Suite 200, Colorado Springs, CO 80920.

Cover by Koechel Peterson & Associates, Minneapolis, Minnesota

MILK & COOKIES TO MAKE YOU SMILE
An expanded version of *Still Lickin' the Spoon*
Copyright © 2002 by Becky Freeman
Published by Harvest House Publishers
Eugene, Oregon 97402

Library of Congress Cataloging-in-Publication Data

Freeman, Becky, 1959-
  Milk and cookies to make you smile/ Becky Freeman.
    p. cm.
  ISBN 0-7369-0648-7 (pbk.)
  1. Religion—Humor. I. Title.
PN6231.R4 F74 2002
200'. 2'07—dc21   2001005968
                                                                                        CIP

Printed in the United States of America.

02 03 04 05 06 07 / BP-VS / 10 9 8 7 6 5 4 3 2 1

To
all the precious children—
and grown-up kids—
who were afraid of the dark on
September 11, 2001.

And in memory of Justin Kalisek,
beloved little brother of our daughter-in-love, Amy.
His childlike grin was the essence of joy.
We will never forget that wonderful boy.

May this book be a hug of hope
to those who long to smile again.

Contents

Acknowledgments

As I finished up edits for the deadline of this book, our world was rocked by explosions of evil on American soil. It seems, suddenly, that all of our grown-up inventions and our grown-up leaders cannot put our lives back together again. And so we run to our Father—a collective nation of vulnerable, hurting children asking Him to hold us and make it all better.

The problems around us are much too big for us to fix; we feel dwarfed by their enormity. The truth is, our problems have always been too big for us.

Abraham Lincoln said, "I have been driven many times to my knees by the overwhelming conviction that I had no where else to go." So now, to our knees we also go—until we receive the calm assurance that the only real safe place for us is snuggled in the hollow of God's hand. He is big enough to hold us, our families, and our future.

How grateful I am for my family; my friends; my agent, Greg Johnson; and my publisher, Harvest House, for re-releasing and allowing me to update and expand my book *Still Lickin' the Spoon* for such a time as this.

I believe they would join me in saying that, at this moment, our greatest gratitude goes to the everyday heroes of our great country, in and out of uniform, who gave—and continue to give—all they had to save the lives of others. "Greater love has no one than this, that he lay down his life for his friends" (John 15:13).

Come unto Me, All You Tired Little Kids
An Invitation to Grow Down

So much has changed since I began writing books about our crazy family some ten years ago. My oldest sons, Zach and Zeke, are out of our cabin-turned-Victorian house and on their own in the big world. Zach just became a father. Zeke is married to lovely Amy. Beautiful, long-legged Rachel is engaged to her handsome prince, Jody. My son, Gabe, the inspiration for my first book, *Worms in My Tea,* has grown from a cute, critter-loving 5-year-old to a handsome, well-muscled athlete of 15. However, as he and his buddies let out whoops and hollers of exaggerated fear as I backed my car out of the high school parking lot yesterday, I realized with a nostalgic smile, *Some things never change.*

● ● ●

Not too long ago I heard a faint knock at my front door and moved to open it. There stood Alex, age two, towheaded with sky-blue eyes, smiling and holding out a branch with some fuchsia berries adorning its leaves.

"I found deese for you, Becky, way off down dere in da woods," he lisped.

Out of the corner of my eye I saw Alex's grandpa, (our neighbor, Wally) standing off in the distance, beaming at his beloved grandchild. My heart melted. *What an honor! A child took the time to stop and share his beautiful treasure with me.*

9

Then I thought again. There was not one child outside my door, but two. For Little Alex and Grandpa Wally are both kids, each in their own special way, each lost in the joy of wonder: Alex, of the branch; Wally, of his grandson.

This knock at the door in the morning, turned into a persistent knocking at my heart by late afternoon. In my mind's eye I saw another dusty day in Jerusalem. A kind man who saw value where others saw nuisance called a child to come stand in a circle of grown-ups. Without hesitation the child bounded toward the man's arms. As this man, Jesus, snuggled the wriggly, grinning little child to Himself, He paused for a second and then looked straight into the eyes of the serious-minded adults around Him. Then He said, in essence, "Guys, if you want to enter into My kingdom, where real life begins and ends, you have a lot to learn from this kid."

What is it? What's the big spiritual secret in their peanut-butter-and-jelly covered faces? What was Jesus trying to tell us about keeping our child-hearts beating, about the key to entering the door of "life more abundant"? Ever hear any sermons on this subject? We hear them on...

- growing up in our faith
- methods of discipleship
- keys to maturity

But how often have you heard a sermon on "growing down"? Or how about "important spiritual disciplines: how to become more like your two-year-old"? There are sermons aplenty about Paul's admonitions to leave childish things behind and press on toward maturity. "Away with the baby food! Bring on the meat!"

But have we thrown out the child with the milk? Have we focused so long on Paul's sermons that we've forgotten to climb into the lap of Christ?

I recently heard an audiotaped message given by Ray Ortlund at a men's conference. At one point he vulnerably confessed, "I sometimes still feel like a kid sucking his thumb, sitting in a giant chair, feet swinging back and forth wondering, 'What in the world is going on?'"

When you read that observation by Mr. Ortlund, what happened inside your heart? I have to admit that I felt an immediate connection to him, a funny sense of relief, and a slow smile of recognition coming to my lips. It was, for me, the turning point in Mr. Ortlund's speech where I went from admiring his wisdom, to thinking, "You know, I really like this guy as a person."

Perhaps Jesus feels the same way about us when we stop trying so hard to figure things out and just crawl into His lap and confess, "Lord, here I am. Just swinging my feet and sucking my thumb. Got any room for me today?"

Strangers sometimes stop me in stores and say, "You look lost. May I help you?" (I think I have a perpetually bewildered look about me.) And whether I am lost or not, I nod because I enjoy the individual, focused attention that being "the little lost child" brings my way. It's akin to the inner longing I feel when I hear the old 40s song "Someone to Watch Over Me." I take care of so many others during the typical course of a day that I long to be watched over, loved, held, soothed, and given kind directions.

Jesus said the words "come unto Me" on two different occasions. Both times He spoke these welcoming words to children, though in one case the children were very small, and in the second case, the *children* lived in tired, grown-up bodies.

To the small kids He said, "Let the little children *come to Me*...for of such is the kingdom of God" (Luke 18:16 NKJV).

And to the big kids He said, "*Come to me,* all you who are weary and burdened, and I will give you rest..." (Matthew 11:28). (Read up a little bit, in verse 25, and you find Jesus referring to His followers as God's "babes" [NKJV]).

Are you more than a little tired of the pressures of having to always be "The Grown-Up in Charge"? Do you long to be "The Little Kid Who Just Trusts and Leans"?

Most of us have spent a lifetime growing up.

How'd you like to take a deep breath, put down your briefcase and car keys, and join me for a bit of growing down?

A little child will lead them.

ISAIAH 11:6

"*It is NEVER too late to have a happy childhood.*"

1

Your Hair Looks Funny!

Unabashed Honesty

liver Wendell Holmes once wrote, "Pretty much all the honest truth-telling in the world is done by children." If you've got a kid under five in your home, you know this to be amazingly accurate...

Except when they are flat-out lying.

But they are so obvious about their fibbing at this age that it's a cinch to detect. When I taught school, my first graders often came in with wild tales of trips to the moon and dinosaurs in their rooms. But if I really wanted to know if my hair looked bad, they were good for the unvarnished truth every time. This innocent honesty is one of the most refreshing and hilariously charming of childhood's attributes.

This reminds me of a scene I wrote a mere seven years ago, when Gabe was in second grade. It captures this burst of childlike honesty I find so disarmingly charming.

Eight-year-old Gabe hugged his side of the car as I swerved to avoid a tree and almost hit a mailbox in the process. (In fact, backing my station wagon out of the driveway is still not my forte. The trees in our yard look like they've been attacked by rabid beavers, so numerous have been my misguided back-ups.)

Our original wagon, The Titanic, which some of you may recall from *Worms in My Tea,* eventually sank— much to our teenagers' delight. For three lovely months I drove an almost-new Ford Explorer. Two small fender benders and a smashing encounter with a Winnebago, however, put me in the driver's seat of this, our current nerd-mobile.

My husband, Scott, believes it is fate. Or God's wrath. Or a twisted joke. There he is, a "sport truck hunk," coupled for all eternity with a "station wagon woman." Even the car's "wood grain" panels are actually sun-faded contact paper.

To add insult to Scott's injury, it also droops down in back like a toddler's too-full diaper. Our older children—Zach, Zeke, and Rachel—appropriately dubbed this car "Sag." But, as Gabe will tell you, "Its real, whole name is Sag, the Tragic Wagon."

The one blessing of driving a station wagon is that there is plenty of metal around me and my kids…and folks can see me coming from afar in time to swerve out of my path.

"Mom?" Gabe asked as he grabbed for the books flying off the seat as I rounded a corner on three-and-a-half wheels.

"Uh, huh," I answered, absently pushing all the wrong buttons as I searched in vain for the radio knob. I knew I was only half-listening to my child, but I simply can't listen to children and operate heavy machinery (like dashboard controls) at the same time. Groping for the radio, I activated the cigarette lighter.

Well, that'll come in handy, I thought, *if I take up smoking in the next ten minutes.* The next button I pressed turned on the windshield wipers. *Wrong again. Not a cloud in sight, and here I am driving down the highway with the wipers waving a warning: Hello! The driver of this car is clueless!*

The next knob sent a stream of water up the front of the windshield.

Well maybe it's a good thing those wipers are in motion after all.

By this time, with my windshield and dashboard in full swing, I could not remember what it was I'd been searching for in the first place. So I flipped on the radio, hoping the music would eventually jar my memory.

That's when I heard Gabe's voice again, seeping into my consciousness.

"Mommm!" He was shouting as he waved a paper napkin in front of my face. Then, carefully enunciating his every word as if I were hard-of-hearing or spoke a foreign language, he said, "Mom! Are - you - pay - ing - *at - ten - tion?*"

"Yes, Gabe. You can put down the flag now. What is it?"

"I was thinking."

"Uh-huh?"

"I was thinking how you are really smart in math and how you write really good books and stuff."

"Well, thank you, Sweetheart."

"But Mom..." he stopped there, a look of concern wrinkling his brow. He glanced up at the wipers methodically smearing hazy twin rainbows of dirty water on the windshield. Then turning his eyes back to me, he finished his proclamation, "Do you know that you have *no sense? At all?*"

There was no animosity in his statement, no trace of sarcasm. He'd just been observing a typical "Mom Scenario" and out popped the conclusion, the cut-and-dried truth. He felt, I suppose, that he should warn me—for my own safety—that my mind, however seemingly intact, should not *ever* be counted on to provide a shred of common, useful sense.

I've known about this mental deficit for a long time, and many others have gently hinted about it through the years. But I'd never heard the truth laid on the line with such blunt accuracy: "Sure, you are smart, Mom. But you have, basically, no sense."

Like the classic tale of the "Emperor and His New Clothes," a child will openly declare the truth everyone else dances around.

● ● ●

My friend Gracie Malone is a true connoisseur of children. As a grandmother of ten with an infectious sense of humor, she keeps the people in our writing circle in stitches with out-of-the-mouths-of-babes stories.

The following e-mail from Grandma Gracie, a classic on the subject of disarming honesty, kept me chuckling off and on for the better of one recent morning.

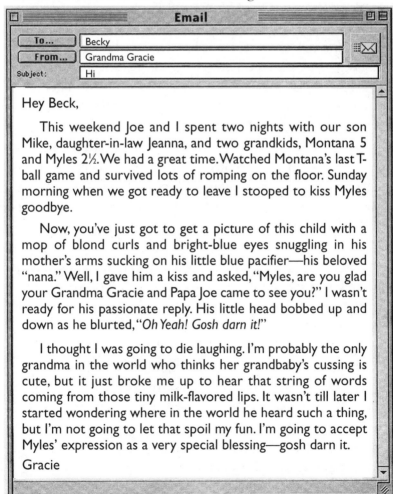

Email

To...	Becky
From...	Grandma Gracie
Subject:	Hi

Hey Beck,

This weekend Joe and I spent two nights with our son Mike, daughter-in-law Jeanna, and two grandkids, Montana 5 and Myles 2½. We had a great time. Watched Montana's last T-ball game and survived lots of romping on the floor. Sunday morning when we got ready to leave I stooped to kiss Myles goodbye.

Now, you've just got to get a picture of this child with a mop of blond curls and bright-blue eyes snuggling in his mother's arms sucking on his little blue pacifier—his beloved "nana." Well, I gave him a kiss and asked, "Myles, are you glad your Grandma Gracie and Papa Joe came to see you?" I wasn't ready for his passionate reply. His little head bobbed up and down as he blurted, "*Oh Yeah! Gosh darn it!*"

I thought I was going to die laughing. I'm probably the only grandma in the world who thinks her grandbaby's cussing is cute, but it just broke me up to hear that string of words coming from those tiny milk-flavored lips. It wasn't till later I started wondering where in the world he heard such a thing, but I'm not going to let that spoil my fun. I'm going to accept Myles' expression as a very special blessing—gosh darn it.

Gracie

On the other end of life's honesty spectrum, I received a call from my 90-year-old friend Vivian Birdwell last night. (She was interviewed and photographed on a jet ski three years ago for my book, *Real Magnolias.* Imagine an adorable elfin woman with wrinkles and the playful eyes of a five-year-old child into mischief.) Her childlike enthusiasm and zest for life always amazes me.

"Becky," Vivian said, "I just called to tell you that I turned 90 this week, and I got 75 presents!"

"My goodness, Vivian!" I exclaimed. "How many people gave you presents?" (I was thinking her family must have doubled and tripled on gift-giving for this special occasion.)

"Why, 75 of course!" she replied. "You should have seen my party!"

I laughed in delight at her obvious joy.

"Are you still living alone? Doing well physically?" I asked.

"Oh, yes. I'm just a blowin' and a goin'. I thank God every day for my good health. I'm still volunteering at God's Open Hand Store, still having the Let's Be Friends Club here every Thursday, and still doing Meals on Wheels."

When I first heard this list of activities, I made the mistake of commenting, "Vivian, I'm so glad you're having someone bring you a meal. You work so hard. You deserve a break!"

Without hesitation, and with no small amount of emphasis, she stated, "Oh, Honey, no. I don't have meals brought to me. I drive for the *elderly.*"

Once Gracie and I were lunching over burritos at Taco Bell with Vivian in her small East Texas town. I was interviewing this feisty, loving lady about life with her husband, who'd died a few years before, and the things she missed about him. I was careful to couch my words gently to avoid painful prodding.

But Vivian would have none of that, diving into the subject with bare hands. And she raised our middle-aged eyebrows as she launched into *all* the things she missed, including the wonderful sexual love the two of them enjoyed for more than 50 years—and how she coped with that loss once he was gone.

(On the way home, Gracie and I mentally calculated the ages of Vivian and her husband, before his death, and determined to ask her on our next trip to see her exactly what vitamins the two of them took.)

Art Linkletter wrote, "I can say, after a lifetime of interviewing, that the two best subjects are children under 10, and folks over 70. Both groups say exactly what's on their minds without regard for the consequences: The kids don't know what they are saying; the old people don't care!"

Could this quality of innocent, unashamed honesty be one of the attributes of childlikeness Jesus loved in human beings? A quality He never meant for us to lose as we grow up? A quality meant to keep us young in heart, mind, and body—even as we age?

To tell you the truth, gosh darn it, I think it is.

You shall know the truth, and the truth shall make you free.

JOHN 8:32 NKJV

2

May I Hold the Baby?

Embracing What Matters Most

Tonight I participated in a scientific experiment. It's something I've not done in nine or ten years, though there was a time when I frequently gathered the necessary drug store supplies and waited with hands wringing or pressed together in prayer for the bathroom/lab results.

Tonight I took a pregnancy test.

I took the test even though my husband, Scott, has had the big "No More Babies" surgery. (The granddaddy of *all* baby-stopping surgeries to hear him tell the tale.)

It also goes without saying that I haven't had a clandestine affair or anything. Besides the fact that I am committed to my husband, I signed a publishing contract stating that my services could be dismissed should I fall into "moral turpitude." (Sounds like paint thinner to me, but I think it's some sort of legal term meaning, "Please don't embarrass us,

unless, that is, you can write it up as family entertainment."
I'm pretty sure that a clandestine affair would be considered
a tad turpitudish.)

Anyway, I was late and when a woman is late she knows
that sometimes, occasionally, the impossible happens.

In case you're holding your breath, the rabbit didn't die.
The criss didn't cross. Nothing and nobody turned blue. I am
still an "I" and not a "we." Looks as though Zach, Zeke,
Rachel, and Gabe will be our Quiver Complete, with no surprise arrows shot our way.

I didn't cry, of course, because the possibility of being
called "Mommy" again had been ridiculous from the start.
Imagine a woman in her late 30s with three teens and a third
grader sitting up nights in a rocking chair, cradling the well-
diapered bottom of a newborn, and patting a cloud-soft
nightie draped over tiny shoulders, as the baby's breath
gently tickles her neck...

Okay, okay. I'll admit it. I've always been a sucker for
babies. Even as a little girl I realized that the infant stage is
rare and precious and fleeting—and then, like puppies, they
soon change into another form not so easily cuddled and
snuggled.

● ● ●

When I was about seven years old, a beautiful, dark-
haired woman at our church gave birth to a beautiful, dark-
haired baby girl. As soon as I spied the mother and baby in
the church nursery, I began praying that someday,
somehow, I'd get to sit next them in a pew.

"And please God," I'd add, "let it be before the baby
grows up and gets too big for a first grader like me to hold."

Then one glorious morning it happened. The young mother sat down, holding the priceless bundle of mysterious sweetness, *right next to me!* I was beside myself, immediately plotting as only a seven-year-old can to take advantage of this once-in-a-lifetime opportunity.

If I can just scoot over close enough I might, could, real gently, touch that soft little baby's head. And if I can make my face look sort of sad and sort of wishing at the same time, the lady might say to me, "Would you like to hold my baby, Becky? After all you're getting to be such a big girl! Why, I can tell just by looking at your face, you're going to make a real good mommy someday."

Yep, that's what she'll probably say. If I look at her just right.

Unfortunately, as hard as I twisted my face with all angst and earnestness, the new mother didn't "read" my facial expressions. I'd have to *verbalize* my longings—a terrifying thought. I was so shy; I rarely spoke to grown-ups other than my parents unless they first spoke to me. However, when it comes to a chance at holding a real, live baby—a little girl's gotta do what a little girl's gotta do.

The last chorus of "Now the Day Is Over" droned to an end as I mentally rehearsed my speech and gathered up my courage. The congregation stirred to leave, the men jingling their keys, the women adjusting their gloves and pillbox hats. I cleared my throat, and it all spilled out in one breathless plea.

"Could I please hold your pretty baby girl for just one minute if I promise cross-my-heart-hope-to-die I won't drop her?"

Thankfully, the mother must have seen the courage it took for a bashful child to blurt out such a heartfelt request. Before I knew it I was holding a real live baby right in the middle of church where everyone could see what a big girl I was. And I knew the entire congregation would be whispering, "Look at that Becky Arnold. What a good little mother she's going to make someday. Do you see how tender she is with that new baby?"

The real baby girl turned out to be much heavier than I'd imagined. Until that moment I'd only rocked two other babies—my stuffed Baby Thumbelina, and my stiff-jointed plastic doll that drank and wet orange Kool-Aid. After the minute had passed, my small arm began to quiver from the weight of the baby's soft-hard head. Still, I loved the warm, breathing, squirmy feel of this live baby doll. When the mother reached for her child, I relinquished my treasure with great reluctance. I had just been given a glimpse of "mommy heaven."

● ● ●

This experience was only surpassed, years later, by the intensity of holding my own real live babies, fresh from my womb. I didn't know I possessed such a fierce protectiveness until I heard my first child cry. Though I was weakened from a long labor, I would have wrestled a samurai to get to my newborn son and quiet his fears.

My beautiful babies...Where did they all go? I look into the eyes of my children now—all of them stretching toward young adulthood—and search for signs of the helpless infants and chubby toddlers they once were. Here and there I catch an occasional glimpse. A lisped word, a mischievous glance, a gentle pat on my shoulder. (Or their complete helplessness and desire for hand-holding when they have the flu.) Does every mother harbor a secret wish that she could bring back her newborns for just an hour or so?

Like Emily, from Thornton Wilder's play *Our Town,* I sometimes wonder, *Do any human beings ever realize life while they live it? Every minute of it? Oh, what I think when I see my youngsters growing up, the precious moments of childhood racing by. How can I squeeze every last second of fun, excitement, and sweetness out of those strange little creatures who are ours for so short a time?*

I look back with gratitude, knowing the first years of my children's lives were savored. I somehow knew that almost everything else tugging at my heart could wait (a career, writing) because these sweet bundles could not. It's also why the housework lay in shambles for most of my ten years of child-bearing, in spite of the "Cleanliness is Next to Godliness" plaque Scott kept trying to nail up on the kitchen wall. (It was pelted so often by toddlers flinging food that I'd have to take it down to clean it.) I cuddled and rocked my babies until their feet dragged the floor, squeezing the joy out of their soft, dimpled presence.

Honestly, now that I've failed the pregnancy test, I'm relieved to be passing up all the pain that comes with an impending birth: swollen ankles, morning sickness, contractions, dirty diapers, confinement, car seats, potty training, runny noses, and every mother's "favorite" plague—chicken pox. As I've stated from the beginning, it would be preposterous for me to cry at this stage of the game over not getting a positive mark on my test.

However, if the crisses had crossed or the dot had turned blue, I'd have found some way to cope with all the child-bearing "downers." Most likely, I'd have dreamed of well-padded baby's bottoms, cloud-soft nighties, and feathery breaths tickling my neck. Even at my age, I might have made a good little mother...just once more.

Oh, pooh, where's a tissue when you need one?

Dishes and dusting can wait till tomorrow

For babies grow up, we've learned to
our sorrow

So quiet down cobwebs, and dust go
to sleep

I'm rocking my baby and babies
don't keep.

—ANONYMOUS

**From the lips of children and infants you have
ordained praise...**

PSALM 8:2

3

Because It's FUN!

Everyday Enjoyments

Early one morning this fall, Zeke slunk in from the back door and gingerly made his way toward the kitchen. Gingerly, I say, because he was dripping wet. And fully clothed. I raised my eyebrows in a silent question as Zeke shook his head and began to chuckle softly to himself. He weakly gathered up the hem of his soggy shirt and wrung some water into the kitchen sink in a futile effort to halt the puddling around him. Then he turned around and looked me full in the face as if to be sure of my undivided attention.

"Mom," he sighed, "you're not gonna believe what Gabe's done this time."

Gabe at age nine is the quintessential "unique" little brother. He is and has always been his own person, what some might even call an odd duck. And speaking of ducks, it was literally an unusual-looking duck that started Zeke on this morning adventure that left him drenched. He had fresh "Gabe news" to report. Diving right in, so to speak, Zeke began his tale.

> Mom, I was sitting out on the dock this morning, watching the sun on the water. You know, just having a few quiet moments to myself before I had to get ready for school. Then I noticed, out on the lake, something kind of funny looking. It looked just like a wounded duck caught in a trotline. So I jumped in and swam toward the bird to see if there was anything I could do to help the poor thing.

He paused for a second, hitching himself up on the kitchen counter where he could deposit his feet in the sink and let the run-off from his jeans drip down the drain.

> Anyway, when I swam out for a closer look, my "wounded duck" turned out to be nothing but an old piece of Styrofoam with a pencil stuck in it. And on the pencil there was a flag with a message in little kid handwriting: "Hi. This is Gabe. I just made this for the fun of it."

Just for the fun of it. Now there's classic "kid reasoning" for you. How often do we grown-ups do something off-the-wall or spontaneous just for the sheer, untarnished fun of it? Probably not often enough. Kids, however, are masters at this.

I ran into a friend of mine, Angie, several years ago. She'd just finished reading *Worms in My Tea* and was bursting with a story to tell me about her young son, Carson, who sounds as though he could be Gabriel's clone.

She said that one afternoon Carson found an earthworm on the back porch and began begging her to come see it right away. But Angie was busy finishing up some vacuuming, so she explained to Carson that she'd come out in a little while.

"Becky," Angie reported, her eyes wide, "you will not believe what I saw when I finally came out to the porch. Carson had been *slinging* that worm around and around like a lariat rope over his head the entire time I'd been vacuuming."

"Oh, no!"

"Oh, yes! And did you know that earthworms *stretch*? I swear that worm was between a foot and 18 inches long by the time I got to it."

"What did Carson say when you asked him why he did it?"

"He told me, 'Mom, I just thought it would be fun to sling a worm.'"

See what I mean? Grown-ups don't think like this. We see some worms and what do *we* do with them? The bravest of us might dig them up and use them for fishing bait. But kids are so much more creative. They think, *Why not let a worm take a swim in a glass of tea? Or better yet, try slinging one?*

● ● ●

The year I taught first grade was a perpetual eye-opener for me in terms of understanding kids' theories on fun: stuffing wads of Play-Doh in their ears, karate-chopping pencils into tiny pieces, cutting designer shapes into their clothing. I'll never forget the afternoon, right in the middle of teaching a lesson, that one little boy—as if jet propelled—abruptly dove out of his desk and landed on the floor at my feet. Later, as we sat in the office together, he innocently explained to the principal, "I sort of thought it would be fun to see how far I could jump out of my seat."

On another occasion, a shy little student walked up to my desk, opened her mouth wide and silently pointed to a button she'd stuck to the roof of her mouth. Neither the school nurse nor I could dislodge it—the suction between her soft palate and the metal button was that strong. Her mother ended up taking this child to the doctor to have it removed! The next day, when I asked my student why she'd stuck the thing up there in the first place, her answer was predictable. "I don't know, Mrs. Fweeman, I just thought it would be fun."

● ● ●

As much as I admire children's penchants for having fun, I realize, as an adult, I must temper my impulses. After all, I don't want to be sitting in a doctor's office with a button stuck on the roof of my mouth or forced to explain a wad of Play-Doh lodged in my ear. Though I've often fantasized about it, I cannot dive out of my seat and onto the floor every time I'm bored with a speaker's presentation. But I think the adult pendulum sometimes swings too far to the "let us behave" side, and we completely forget what it's like to have good, wholesome fun for fun's sake.

In an effort to bring more fun into my life, I recently purchased a book called *Ten Fun Things to Do Before You Die*. It was written, believe it or not, by a Catholic nun, Karol A. Jackowski. Now this sister has a few quirky beliefs, but overall she seems like a pretty fun nun, the sort I'd love to meet for coffee and conversation. (Why do I keep envisioning Whoopi Goldberg?) After 42 years of living, Sister

Jackowski declares she's found four ways to "have more fun than anyone else."

The first piece of advice she gives is to find fun people. Apparently, this is not an easy trick. Sister Karol writes, "One of the hardest things to find in life is fun people. Far too few appear and seemingly fewer survive adulthood." Suggested things to watch for on a search for fun people are "good storytelling, perfect timing, interesting work, a good appetite, unusual sense of humor, fresh insight, and a brave, daring life."

Advice number two is "forget about yourself around other people. Not to do so is…just plain rude." I like this one; it's especially freeing to a self-centered person such as myself. Mother and I laughed the other day about how we sometimes feel burdened to entertain other people whenever we are in group situations—as if it is our obligation to provide the floor show or something. "Not necessary," Karol says. "A good general rule is to think about yourself when you're by yourself and in the presence of others, think and ask about them."

Third, she writes, "Be a fun person." To do this you must make yourself interesting and be on the watch for opportunities that have the potential for great fun. Opportunities like "Clyde Peeling's Reptile Farm off the Pennsylvania Turnpike, any Dairy Queen, and, yes, boring meetings."

There are limits to fun. But not many. The "Fun Nun" says, "If it looks like fun and doesn't break the Ten Commandments—do it." Sounds like a good rule of nun…I mean thumb…to me.

On a recent country getaway with a group of women from my church, I found myself gravitating toward one woman in particular. Right from the start Terry exhibited all the signs of being a fun person. In the course of conversation, we discovered Terry had traveled down the Amazon, gotten lost in South America, and barely escaped a guerrilla's spray of machine gun fire. She'd also been a full-fledged hippie—her wedding taking place in a field of flowers. And though Terry has grown into a respectable Bible study leader, she's not finished being daring and interesting yet. Before the night was out, she handed each of us a drinking straw and with great gusto announced, "I am going to teach you all a new skill—one you can use to totally amaze and impress your kids or even strangers in restaurants."

Then, with all the dignity she could muster, Terry placed one end of the straw in her mouth and secured the other end—very carefully—into her armpit. Then she blew. For a few seconds we all sat motionless, stunned at the disgusting noises arising from the crevices in Terry's arm...and grateful we were not, at the moment, in a public place. But within seconds, we all began scrambling like crazy for our own straws to try the trick on ourselves. Before I indulged, however, I mentally went over the Ten Commandments. When I could not find a deeply spiritual reason to abstain, I went ahead and blew for all I was worth. I only wish my teenage sons could have seen me in such top form. They would have been so proud. For reasons I cannot begin to explain, it was one of the most spontaneous, fun evenings I've ever had with a group of women.

Postscript: At a lovely publisher's dinner surrounded by quiet, dignified Canadian businessmen (yawwwnnn...) I decided to brave telling them about this trick with the challenge, "Try this at home."

The next day, at the Toronto bookseller's convention, I was surrounded by several laughing, smiling Canadians who could not wait to tell me about the fun they'd been having with their kids. (Yes, Virginia, Canadians do smile, but only if provoked.) Go ahead—pick up some straws for family dinner tonight!

● ● ●

I love the story from the Gospels where we find Jesus telling Martha, Mary's compulsive-cleaning sister, to "chill out, leave the dishes alone, and come sit a spell with Me." (This is, by the way, my own very loose translation.) He wanted Martha to get in on the fun conversation while she had a chance. After all, it wasn't every day that Jesus would be stopping by. The dishes could wait. Special opportunities may not.

As I was writing this very chapter one sunny Sunday afternoon, I had not just one, but *two* girlfriends call and ask me to go out to play. What's a fun girl with a hovering deadline and a room full of dirty laundry to do?

I glanced up from the story of Mary and Martha, and informed my husband Scott, "It's obviously the will of God that I go."

So I ended up in Dallas, soaking up sun on a quilt with my two friends. We were each eating a smoked ear of corn on the cob that was dripping with butter and covered with sour cream and bacon bits (to die for!).

Between stuffing ourselves and girl gabbing, we also watched magnificent, brightly colored hot air balloons take off, one after another. With corn between my teeth and sour cream around my mouth, I grinned at my friends and slowly drawled, "I don't know about you guys, but I think this beats bleaching socks all to pieces."

That spring afternoon, my family ended up eating sandwiches and doing their own laundry. But what my husband

and children got out of the deal was a wife and mother who came home smiling and refreshed and happy to be alive. They agreed it was a pretty good trade-off. And obviously, if you are reading this, I made my deadline.

● ● ●

Once I started looking for the fun, it took on a life of its own. I was getting my hair highlighted, which meant at one point I had to wait 20 minutes with pieces of my hair jutting out from my head, wrapped in aluminum foil. I looked like an alien who'd just landed in a beauty shop. Realizing I had 20 minutes to kill, and that I had some letters to mail, and that the post office was just next door—I looked in the mirror, smiled, and decided to go for the run. Why not? I got my letters mailed and, trust me, I made the mailman's day.

So I say, "Sail that Styrofoam boat! Get that dusty kite out of the closet and go fly it for all it's worth! Ride a hot air balloon, eat greasy fair food, blow silly noises through straws, and walk around town with Reynold's-wrapped hair!"

Do something each day on which you can look back and say, "I did that for the sheer, simple, childlike *fun* of it.

You, and all heaven, will smile!

God...richly provides us with everything for our enjoyment.

1 TIMOTHY 6:17

Becky's Fun Mottos to Live By

"If you always wait 'til your chores are done, you'll never ever have any fun."

"Sometimes the sun shines from the outside in, sometimes it has to shine from the inside out."

4

I'm Just Grinnin'

A Cheerful Countenance

So. Scott and I have finally done it. We've graduated from preschool.

Well, actually, it is our *children* who have graduated from preschool. We, more accurately, have officially completed all required labs in Preschool Parenting. Funny, this new stage. As I've already admitted, there is a certain melancholy in bidding farewell to the childbearing, toddler-chasing years. But have I mentioned the waves of euphoria that also come with this time of transition?

There is something akin to giddiness in knowing that never again will it be *my* candy-crazed toddler having the rabid-like breakdown on Grocery Aisle B. Not only that, but Scott and I are now free to spoil "other people's children" with nary a thought to the consequences. We get to be like fairy godparents to our young nieces and nephews and neighborhood children. We're perpetual nice guys.

There are three little preschoolers down the street whose standard greeting to us is, "Do you have a treat for me today?" Scott, especially, almost always has a stick of gum or a piece of candy ready for just such occasions. If only real parenting were as easy as handing out goodies.

I remember when our son Zachary was about 18 months old. My Aunt Hazel came for a visit. Before long Zach started in with some well-timed whining and foot stomping around the vicinity of Aunt Hazel's knees. Her automatic response to his fit of passion was to kiss him on the forehead and place two gooey cookies in his dimpled hands. I started to give her that don't-spoil-him look, but before I could say anything Hazel slapped her hand on the counter and matter-of-factly said, "Becky, how would you like my advice on raising children?"

"Sure," I replied, eager for any help I could glean at this stage of the game.

"Okay, here it is: Give them everything they want; don't ever say no."

I smiled as I raised my eyebrows. "Is this the method you used to raise your son?"

"Of course not. It's my advice on how you should raise my great-nephew."

Now that I'm an auntie myself, I'm free to adopt Aunt Hazel's child-rearing advice—to be used only with other people's children, of course. Take, for example, my nephew Tyler.

First of all, I should explain that Tyler glows. There is no other word to appropriately describe this child phenomenon. By "glowing" I mean when this kid smiles, he smiles all over. The grin that starts at the corners of his mouth spreads out like ripples of water to his dimpled cheeks, moving upward to his eyebrows causing them to pop up and down with excitement, the lights fairly dancing in his eyes below. Giggles flow freely, not only from his mouth, but seemingly from every joint in his body. Tyler is also very small for his age. When he was six years old, on his first summer visit to "Aunt Becky's Country Cabin," he really looked more like a child of about four, so small and elfinlike was he.

Because of his size, I'm always picking him up, without thinking, and loving on him as I would a toddler. When I first saw him last summer, I ran to him, and lifted him off the floor in a huge bear hug.

He was polite. He even managed to give his crazy Aunt Becky an obligatory pat on the back. But I was startled when I heard his very grown-up voice over my shoulder insisting, "Aunt Becky, I'd like you to put me down now. I was about to go work on the computer."

Tyler's mother, Barbara, is one of those wonderfully organized mothers. Before Tyler's visit, she called me from their home in Indiana to fill me in on his routine. (My brother David had driven Tyler down to stay with us while he did some fishing in nearby East Texas bass lakes.)

"Becky," she said, as always, distinctly enunciating her words, "Tyler usually goes to bed at 8:00 P.M., and it is very important that he do some schoolwork while he is there so he won't get behind in his studies. I'll pack a fresh change of clothes and underwear for every day—you know how picky he is about staying clean. He knows how to brush and floss his own teeth, of course. And he really shouldn't have too much sugar or junk food because it tends to make him hyper."

Barb, I hope you will forgive me. I must confess that it only took one week under my watchful care for her son to go completely to pot. Somehow we never got around to the homework. I have no recollection of the toothbrush. (However, I do think we used the floss for emergency fishing line.) And don't even ask me about the condition of his underwear. The only thing I'm sure that Tyler changed was his affinity for staying neat and clean. But we did manage to have some big-time fun.

For days on end, Tyler fished down at our lake pier to his heart's content (and Tyler's "heart's content" averages about eight hours of casting and catching a day). In this area of intense interest, he is his daddy's own son. I remember when my brother was about his son's age and dug a huge hole in our suburban backyard. After filling it up with water from the hydrant, he sat for hours certain that at any minute he'd snag a whopper. (I'm sure our mother thought the hole in the backyard was well worth a few days of peace and quiet.) Our local paper even snapped a picture of David fishing at a nearby pond. He was holding three cane poles at once in his small, clasped hands.

During most of Tyler's stay with us, he only set his pole down long enough to call up to the house for fresh rations of peanut-butter-and-jelly sandwiches. Oh, and he'd yell for a jacket when the sun began to fade and the evening air took on a chill.

If Barb had seen her son at the end of a typical day at our home, I don't know if she'd ever let him come back. (She tells me she'd just rather not know.) Basically, Tyler turns into a grimy ball of worm slime with fragrant splashes of perch and crappie lingering about his hands. However, he could never get dirty or smelly enough to cover his glow.

And so, when he flashed his big grin and asked me to take him to the store for fresh minnows, I rarely (if ever) said no.

On the way home from such a trip to Gantt's Village minnow/deli/convenience store, I happened to glance in my rearview mirror toward the back of the station wagon. There sat Tyler, all grins, a chicken leg in one hand and a lollipop in the other. He was contentedly alternating fists with bites and licks. It was awfully cute, but I was soon lecturing myself.

> *Now Becky, you are spoiling this child just because he's your nephew and he happens to be adorable. You've got to quit being such a gullible old softy. What will you tell Barb? That he ate balanced meals because he always had food of equal weight in both hands?!*

Late one evening, shortly thereafter, I realized things were totally out of control. Wandering into the kitchen I found Tyler perched on a stool behind the counter. This was obviously a kid on a mission. He'd taken two half gallons of Blue Bell ice cream out of the freezer and positioned one on either side of himself. (If you don't know about Blue Bell, just find any transplanted Texans in your area, ask them about it, and watch their eyes glaze over with wonder.)

The lids were off both cartons and Tyler held a spoon in each hand, poised for action. I started to protest, but then he looked up at me, his face lit up like a Fourth of July sky.

"Man, I love this place!" he declared, "I've had ice cream for supper two nights in a row now."

Okay, I know it's awful. But I can't help it. I just can't find it in my heart to say no to a child who's about to glow. Besides it was only one week out of a year; how much harm can one little week of nonstop sugar and worm dirt do to a kid?

This fall, David and Barb allowed Tyler to come for one more visit. As they were making preparations for this second trip out, Barb called ahead. She was as nice as she could be, but I could tell she was still struggling to recover from Tyler's last visit with us.

"Hi, Becky," she said, "just wanted to go over Tyler's routine. Again." (How can I blame her? She must have been thinking, *Let's try this once more*—with feeling.

"Oh, Barb," I apologized, "I'm sorry we got Tyler so off schedule last time. You know how crazy things get around here. By the way, did you get the package I mailed after he left?"

"Yes," she answered with measured calmness, "and I really do appreciate you mailing Tyler's homework back. I understand you finally found his workbook in the back of your station wagon under the minnow bucket. Actually, that's sort of what I was calling about. Since we are taking Tyler out of school for the week, do you think you could encourage him to actually *write* something on the worksheets this time? Fill in some blanks, underline a sentence, and circle something? I don't care if he stays clean. I can even handle digging the worm dirt out of his pockets when he gets back home. And a week without flossing won't cause his teeth to rot out. But if he can just do some homework this time—all I ask is the *homework*."

I tried to give Barb my most reassuring response, but I was soon distracted because I could hear Tyler's humming somewhere in the background.

"Barb," I said, "let me talk to Tyler a second."

"Okay," she responded, and I could hear her calling to Tyler to come say "hi" to his Aunt Becky. But Tyler was too busy.

"Tell Aunt Becky I'm just not in the mood," I could hear my nephew's voice ring out in the background. (Tyler picked up perfect diction from his mother, so there was no mistaking his answer.) Then, as an afterthought, I heard him add, "But tell her to be ready to whip out the Blue Bell when I get there!"

What can I say? I rushed right out for a carton of Vanilla Bean and one of Cookies and Cream.

When Tyler arrived at our house this time, he felt easily at home, settling into a routine right away. (In other words, he didn't open his suitcase for the first two days.) One afternoon, when it was raining too hard to fish, Tyler sat and watched a Power Robo Something cartoon on TV. In response to the action on the television, he abruptly yelled out, "Awesome!"

"What's awesome?" I quizzed from the kitchen.

"Nothing," came the serious voice, followed by a heavy sigh from the living room. "I'm sorry, you're too old to understand."

Well, perhaps he is right. (I believe Oscar Wilde once said, "I am not young enough to know everything.") But this much I do understand. Tyler most definitely has the upper hand in our relationship. Even his insults seem cute to me these days.

Toward evening that same day, my happy but exhausted nephew crawled up in my arms and fell asleep on my lap. When my brother walked in the door to take his son back home, I looked down at Tyler's sleeping form, then back up at David. On reflex, I asked, "Can I keep him, huh, can I keep him?" David chuckled, strolled over to stroke his son's hair, looked at me gently, and shook his head no. It was a painful goodbye.

But good news! I am going to see Tyler again soon. This time we'll meet in Virginia where the whole clan is gathering at my sister's for Christmas. I only have one problem. How am I going to transport two half-gallons of Blue Bell ice cream on the airplane? (My editor, who happens to be a transplanted Texan, yielded the answer to my dilemma. She says an Igloo and dry ice work nicely.)

What am I thinking? If I'm considering going to these lengths to spoil my nephew, can you imagine me as a *grandma* someday? I wonder if there is a Continuing Ed course called "How to Say No to Children Who Glow."

As I was pondering Tyler's glowing charm and my tendency to give in to anything he wants, I came across an intriguing quote by Winston Churchill. As you know, Churchill was one of history's ultimate charmers. I believe I have some insight into his ability to wrap the free world around his chubby little finger. One day he seriously intoned, "We are all worms." And then with childlike confidence and a gleam in his eye he added, "But I do believe that I am a glowworm."

In life, especially as we grow older, we are faced with two choices. Either we can resign ourselves to growing old and dull, or we can find ways to light up the world with humor and smiles—thereby attracting others into our circle of delight.

We might as well go for the glow!

Those who are wise will shine...

DANIEL 12:3

5

I'm So Sorry, Frog!

Tenderheartedness

Driving in the car one night, Gabe's little buddy Dallas was relating a scene from the recent *Little Rascals* movie.

"See, the Little Rascals had this 'He-Man, Women-Hater's Club.' And the kid with the real deep voice, the one they call Froggie, was telling his friends about a girl that had played a mean trick on him. But he got back at her. He took out a lizard and showed it to that *girl!*"

Dallas thought this was so funny he was laughing out loud even before he finished the tale. Gabe sat in the back seat, completely blank-faced.

"So?"

"So, it scared her."

"Why?"

"Because girls are scared of lizards."

"Why?"

"Because they just are."

"That's not true. I know lots of girls who like lizards. If somebody showed me a lizard, I'd reach out and pet it. I'd love it!"

After all these years, it is still incomprehensible to Gabriel that any sane person could dislike a reptile or an amphibian. Like the title of Arnold Lobel's famous children's book states, *Frog and Toad Are Friends*. And according to Gabriel, they are our friends.

Though much of Gabe's amphibian/reptile-loving history has already been well documented, the stories continued to abound until Gabe hit puberty at age 11. And then, finally, frogs and snails and puppy dog tails took a backseat to girls, sports, and styling gel.

Even at age nine, Gabe was as critter-loving a kid as I've ever seen. On his desk during that third-grade year, I counted two turtles, one frog, two hermit crabs and—oh yes, about a dozen tadpoles swimming in (what else?) my best crystal bowl. I put up with a lot, when it comes to matters of the heart. And for Gabe, frogs and turtles and tadpoles and such are definitely affairs of the heart.

● ● ●

Once, just once, in an effort to be "cool," Gabe broke his own little frog-loving heart. And I'll never forget it. That fateful afternoon, Gabe burst into the house and dived onto my bed, wrapping a sheet tightly around his head. Being the sensitive and observant mother that I am, I knew right away something must be amiss.

"Gabriel," I coaxed, "what's the matter, Honey?"

Nothing. No response from under the covers.

"Gabe, you can tell me *anything*. Have you done something wrong?"

There was a slight movement in the affirmative from the mummified form.

"Well, there's nothing you've done that can't be forgiven. Come on out and let's talk."

When he finally unraveled himself from the sheets, I was taken aback by the flood of tears on his face and the obvious agony of soul in his eyes.

"What, Honey, what?" I asked softly, shaking my head and searching his face for clues.

After a few gulps he finally managed to say, "I… gigged…a…frog."

"Oh, dear," I said, remembering that Gabe's big brothers had been into gigging bullfrogs for sport and then cooking their "game" for meat—the legs, that is. I'd never approved of it, but I know boys will be boys and tried not to think about the "frog hunting" going on in nearby ponds.

And now it was clear: Gabe, trying to be a big hunter like his brothers, had taken a kitchen fork and "gigged" a small frog, thinking he'd bring home fresh "game" like the big guys.

"Oh, Gabriel," I said, swallowing a lump in my throat, "did it surprise you when you realized you had hurt something you've always loved?"

"Mo—o—mmm," he sobbed into my shoulder, his small fingers squeezing tightly into my arms, "I didn't think about it hurting him until it was over!"

I found myself fighting my own tears while I was trying to convince my son he could be forgiven for his mistake.

"I'm so sorry! I didn't mean to do such a sad, sad thing. I didn't know it would hurt you this bad!"

In truth, I wasn't stifling a tear for Gabe's heinous crime. It was because I identified with him so much. Have we not all, at one time or another, hurt something we loved and held dear? Haven't I gigged the ones I love the most with my careless or hateful words? And then suffered the weight of my guilt—wishing so hard that I could turn back the clock and erase something awful I'd said or done? Every child, every man, and every woman has at one time or another, come face-to-face with the fact that they've just gigged an innocent frog.

That is, if they are still tenderhearted enough to admit it. We can so easily become calloused, but tenderheartedness is one of the most precious childlike qualities God asks us to cherish on into adulthood....But I digress. Back to the frog tragedy before us.

What's a mother to do in the face of such angst and repentance?

Dry the tears. Have a proper burial. (Where, in desperation to comfort my son, I stretched all theological lines making up incredible stories about green clouds and froggie heaven.)

Then we go back to loving frogs—this time with a deeper awareness of how precious and dear and inescapably beautiful are all the things that have been created by God's hand.

A few months after the frog-gigging crisis, Gabe and I were walking hand in hand along our country road. Out from the woods, a box turtle lumbered into view. Gabe looked up at me and grinned toward heaven.

"Oh, wow, Mom," he said reverently. "That's *two*."

"Two what?" I asked, peering down at his upturned face.

"That's two turtles in one day! Man, God sure has been good to me."

(From this anecdote emerged a family motto. Any really great day, one of double blessings, is now and forever known as a Two Turtle day.)

With the sighting of those turtles, Gabe knew, as only a child can know, that all had been forgiven—for God smiles on the kind and tenderhearted, even though we sometimes blow it big time.

Postscript: You may not believe this, but it's true! As I was typing in the last sentence of this chapter, a huge box turtle, one I've never seen before, crawled out from under my desk and lumbered across my carpeted floor.

Maybe there *is* an amphibian heaven....

Be gentle and ready to forgive; never hold grudges. Remember, the Lord forgave you, so you must forgive others.

Colossians 3:13 TLB

In Praise of Tender Hearts
(or "Ode to a Toad")

When will the gigging stop
and clean forgiveness flow
from tender hearts
so wounds might heal?
Or must we go on washing hands
of those we once embraced?
How sad, how tragic—
a calloused heart.
Beware, the heart that turns to stone
safe, protecting stone.
For know
the stone
in time
becomes
a tomb.
The children are the wise
for of such is—yes!—
the kingdom.
Oh, choose the childlike
tender heart.
Hope all things
Unguarded be
Mourn the pain
of human clay
Choose to be hurt
that we might
love—then rise,
again, to Life!*

* Becky Freeman, © 1997.

6

Angels Watchin' Over Me

Trust in the Unseen

Those of you who've been involved in an accident or have survived a trauma of some kind know how dreamlike and unreal such situations can seem at the time they occur. My good friend Deborah Morris writes true-life dramas for a living. (Check out her website: www.realkids.com.) One day as we were visiting over a cup of coffee, I asked Deb if she had noticed any particular similarities among the stories she'd heard from trauma survivors. I found her reply fascinating.

"Becky," Deborah said, pausing to set down her cup, "out of the dozens of people I've interviewed, almost all of them report that during the actual crises, everything begins to take on a surreal quality. I also find it interesting that accident victims most often do not experience a huge amount of fear or pain during the traumatic event. It's as if a peaceful heaven-sent anesthetic is delivered, for a brief time, until they are gradually pulled back into reality and the coping process begins."

I know from personal experience that this is true. And I find it of no small comfort, since I have a passionate dislike for pain. I'm not afraid of death, mind you. Death I can handle. I'm actually looking forward to my "home going" someday. But suffering, misery, and agony—the trappings so often associated with death—I can't say I'm looking forward to these. Death and heaven, fine. Death and writhing agony, not so good. However, I'm not as nervous about pain as I used to be, at least not the initial pain of trauma. And there's something else, too. I believe God sends ministers—angels—to comfort us in times such as these.

So I offer my own story to add to the testimonies of countless others, a short story of shock, of relief, and of the whisper of angels' wings. A story that affirms all over again the words of the song that has soothed many a child (and many a grown-up) down through the years: "All night, all day, angels watchin' over me."

● ● ●

It happened in the spring as Gabe and I were pulling out of a convenience store parking lot and onto the highway. Unable to see around an 18-wheeler parked in front of the store, I slowly inched the nose of my Ford Explorer onto the shoulder of the highway until I could get a clear view. The driver of a Winnebago, who was going about 65 miles an hour, could not see me inching out behind the semi.

At the moment of impact, Gabe was fastening his seat belt. My seat belt was already fastened—probably a lifesaver, since the driver's side took the blow. When everything came to a screeching halt, our new (new to us, anyway) Explorer's entire front end was smashed beyond recognition. The highway patrolman told us later that if we'd been hit a few inches farther back, Gabe and I could not have survived. Just the memory of the car—with the entire hood lying like a crumpled drape over to one side—sends a chill up my spine.

Fortunately, large RVs are mostly constructed of foam and fiberglass. As I understand it, they are basically Styrofoam coolers—like the ones you get at 7-11—only bigger and on wheels. A few hunks of Winnebago flew down the highway, but thankfully, the nice older couple inside was unharmed. A vehicle of heftier construction would have done considerably more damage to our Explorer and, in turn, to us.

What I found so odd, after it was all over, was how calm things had been inside our car at the moment of impact, and how unreal it all seems even now to Gabe and me. Thankfully, Gabe came away unscathed, although he remains especially skittish at intersections. ("Mom, are you sure our car's nose isn't sticking out too far?") I came away with a large "goose egg" on my head and a cut and bruise on my leg. Surprisingly I didn't feel either injury at all the moment they occurred. I felt no impact, no pain whatsoever. I find that simply incredible!

You see when I whack my head on the corner of the kitchen cabinet—I know it. Immediately. When I step on a piece of glass I yelp ASAP. But it was a good 15 minutes after Gabe and I were escorted to safety before I felt *any* pain of any sort anywhere. I wondered at the time, *Is this that accident numbing thing Deb talked about?* Then another question popped into my mind. *Well, obviously it was not our time to die, so did God use angelic intervention to keep my son and me from serious harm?*

I've often joked about the two angels who ride shotgun on my bumpers as I meander down country roads. (A friend of mine once told me her son, Jake, said, "Mom, I know angels are real 'cause grandma has two wooden ones right on her desk.") But I've quit joking about angels so much. In fact, I think I may have "met" one of my angels that day.

After the policemen had gone and the crowd cleared away, I was left alone for a few minutes sitting on a bench in front of the convenience store, holding an ice pack to my head. Big Brother Zachary had arrived earlier and taken over the care and feeding of Gabriel. With his money, Zach bought his little brother a large soft drink and two huge candy bars. From the look on Gabe's chocolate-covered face, I could see the sweets had greatly helped to ease his pain. Together they went next door to retell and expound the drama to some of their friends.

As I was sitting there, numb and dazed and offering thanks to God for the sparing of our lives, a van pulled into the vacated parking lot. A large man—mid-fiftiesh, nice-looking—stepped out of the vehicle's door and walked straight to where I was sitting.

"Hello," he said kindly. "I was just driving down the road, and I felt God telling me I needed to stop and tell you something."

I was beginning to feel a little woozy at that point and thought, *This is really a weird day.* The day was strange, but I certainly wanted to hear whatever it was God might have to say through this man. Believe me, the Almighty had my full attention that morning. When I spoke, my voice was still a little shaky.

"It was nice of you to stop," I responded. "Did you see the accident?"

"No," answered the man, smiling. I looked over near the road and remembered the Explorer had already been towed away by the scruff of what was left of its neck to the home for smashed cars. The man continued, his voice deep and soothing.

"No, I just saw you sitting here." He paused as if wanting to make sure he had his message just right. "I want to tell you that God loves you very much. And though you may not understand why this happened, He wants you to know He cares."

"Thank you," I said, a strong sense of comfort and calm rising inside me. This "heavenly telegram" from out of nowhere was oddly reassuring. It was so simple, but it was everything I needed to hear. It was a reminder that my Father is personally concerned, even while—maybe even *especially when*—the whole world's gone haywire.

The man returned to his van, and my thoughts drifted to all the many friends and strangers who had come to our aid that morning as soon as they saw or heard what had happened. How kind they were, and how blessed I was to have their help. Even the highway patrolman was exceptional. And, my, it was awfully good to breathe in and out and move and be alive and hold my son who, though shaken, was at least still in one piece. And now this, a perfect stranger taking time to stop and offer words of encouragement.

Until that morning and the sound of crunching steel on steel, I'd been heady with excitement over my "new" creamy-gold Explorer. It was the only nice car I'd ever owned, and I only had it three-and-a-half months before the big crunch. Yet even as its crumpled body was being hauled away, I realized that car meant nothing to me in light of what had occurred. *Absolutely nothing.* Cars can be replaced.

My thoughts returned to my "visitor," and my gaze followed the van now rounding a bend in the road until it disappeared from sight. *I wonder if that van driver is spreading his wings and flying back to heaven right now?* Angelic or human, it doesn't really matter. The message he bore was truly heaven sent.

● ● ●

Soon after the accident, my lifelong friend and cousin Jamie called with a story about her youngest child, four-year-old Martha—little Martha who is a delicate, sweet, and shy little girl with soft blonde hair and beautiful blue eyes and an adorable way of talking.

Jamie and her mother (Martha's grandmother) had taken Jamie's four young children along on a shopping trip to a mall in Houston. When they were pooped out, they stopped to rest a moment near the bottom of an escalator. As kids will do, little Martha leaned her arms over the escalator's handrail, as she stood on the floor beside it watching people going up, up, up—20 feet to the next level.

As the railing rose, Martha also lifted her feet off the ground for a ride. Before anyone knew what was happening, her small body began rising above the mall floor. She was dangling on the outside of the stairs being held only by her tiny arms clinging to the handrail. It all happened so fast that by the time Jamie looked up, screamed, and began sprinting up the steps to help her daughter, it was too late. When Martha reached the top—20 feet above the ground—she hit the second floor wall. Her grandmother watched in helpless horror as she saw one little hand let go and then the other.

And that's when I imagine Martha's guardian angel got to work. A woman standing below the escalator happened to see what was going on, positioned herself, said a silent prayer for strength, and opened her arms. As Martha fell from the second story, the woman made a successful catch. Both woman and child went down with the impact, but thankfully both were unhurt. (Of course, they were stunned.)

Martha lay there in the woman's lap on the floor, perfectly still, not saying a word. Nothing seemed hurt, but she might have been in shock—or experiencing that "accident-numbing thing." After a long while, she wriggled and tugged at her rescuer's shirt. The woman leaned down closer to hear the quiet little voice. In the midst of noise and turmoil and Jamie's crying and the grandmother's sighs of relief, Martha had one concern on her ladylike four-year-old mind.

"My unduhweauh is showing," she whispered.

See that you do not look down on one of these little ones. For I tell you that their angels in heaven always see the face of my Father in heaven.

MATTHEW 18:10

7

Aren't I Cute?

Childlike Charm

My friend and next-door neighbor, Melissa, has a daughter named Sarah. We tease Melissa by saying that Sarah acts more like she's *my* daughter than Melissa's child. Though Sarah's a blue-eyed, cherub-faced, blonde and I'm an olive-skinned brunette, I must admit we have a lot in common. Our best hope of survival in this world—other than the ever-abiding presence of our guardian angels—is our ability to be really cute once we get ourselves into hot water.

● ● ●

Since Sarah's overactive conscience sometimes makes her honest to a fault, it is vital that she maintains her charm as she begins her truth telling. Otherwise, one might be tempted to wring her neck.

One April afternoon about six years ago, the phone rang. I answered and heard Sarah's cheerful voice on the other end of the line.

"Happy birthday, Becky!" she said.

"Oh, Sarah—how nice of you to remember!" I responded with genuine feeling.

"Well, I *didn't* remember." As I said, from Miss Sarah, one can always expect the unvarnished truth. I thought I'd help ease her conscience.

"It's okay, Sarah. You didn't remember yesterday, on my actual birthday—but you remembered today, and it was so nice of you to call."

"Well...we didn't actually remember today or yesterday. Gabe just told us about it."

I was determined to be gracious about these belated birthday greetings, but Sarah was not making it easy.

"Okay, Sarah, but you see the fact is you called to wish me a happy birthday *all on your own,* and that was a very nice thing to do. Thank you."

A loud silence followed. The angst on the end of the line was palpable, for Sarah is always compelled to tell the whole truth and nothing but the truth.

"Well, actually..." Sarah started.

I gave up. There would be no stopping Sarah until she had completely unburdened herself.

"Well, actually, Gabe *made* me call."

I could see it was important that I get the complete and absolute truth. Sarah was indeed telephoning me with a heartfelt and sincere-sounding birthday greeting. However, she felt (who knows why?) that I must understand that my young son was forcing her to do so. (I could only pray at this point that he wasn't holding her hostage.)

Anxious to put an end to this conversation before more true confessions poured across the line, I signed off in a hurry.

"Sarah, thanks for calling. You have made my day."

"Oh, you're welcome," came the sweet reply.

● ● ●

Not only are Sarah's "live" phone calls entertaining, the ones she leaves on my answering machine are equally popular. And they bear permanent testimony to her confused state of mind, with which I identify so heartily. When someone says, "Sarah left another message!" we all come running to hear it. For one thing, it took little Sarah a couple of tries to figure out that my voice on the other end was actually a tape recording and not Becky-in-person. How did we know?

Well, her first recorded phone message went something like this.

> Can Gabe come over? What are you saying to me? Momma! Come here! Becky just picked up the phone, and started talking to me, and I don't understand anything she said. What? Oh. Is this a recording? Oh. Well I just don't know what to say. I guess I'm just pretty mixed up.

There was another famous "Sarah" message I almost couldn't bring myself to erase. It was left during the summer while Gabe was supposed to have been over at her house playing. I later learned he had run home to go to the bathroom, but he'd neglected to tell Sarah he was leaving. When

I checked the phone recorder later, I noticed the message light was blinking. Sarah very seriously started talking.

> Becky, I'm sorry to tell you this but I lost Gabe. I can't find him anywhere. I'm sorry. He was here and now he is gone, and I've looked everywhere. I don't know what else to do. We just lost him, that's all. I'm sorry, but he's gone. That's all I can say. I am really, really sorry.

Ah, a girl after my own befuddled heart. Thankfully, if you know how to play your charm cards right, even confusion and mix-ups can endear others to you. (And vice-versa.)

Once again, I can relate to Sarah's message. If there is one underlying theme running through my own psyche, it is this: I am sorry. I am sorry I'm late. I'm sorry dinner isn't on the table right now. Or in the oven. Or even in little unprepared segments in the refrigerator. I'm sorry the house is a mess, and I'm sorry I've gained five more pounds. However, I am a sorry survivor. Let me rephrase that. I am a survivor of sorry.

● ● ●

How? I work really, really hard at being cute enough to compensate. Sometimes it does the trick, sometimes it backfires. But if you happen to be a child like Sarah or an adult like me—if you find yourself being too honest for your own good, if you are perpetually perplexed, or if you have a hard time keeping up with important things (like eight-year-old boys)—you may want to take careful notes because I recently pulled off a coup de cute, and it probably saved my skin.

One afternoon I was rummaging through the trash can that is my purse, and I came upon a tissue-thin piece of paper I'd forgotten all about. It happened to be a traffic ticket I'd received while driving on one of Gabe's field trips a few weeks earlier. It was a ticket for running a stop sign at the park. Upon examining the fine print, I realized with some shock that I had missed the court date by a full ten days.

Since Scott had recently bent another woman's fender, and I had a recent major accident claim on my insurance, a thought occurred to me: *Maybe this is not the best time to have an outstanding warrant for my arrest.*

When I confessed my error to my husband, his expression didn't change—the way Clint Eastwood's doesn't change—and he retired to our bedroom to meditate. When he came out, his speech was prepared.

"Becky, listen. This problem could be disastrous. With another ticket, the insurance company could drop us and put us into an insurance pool for high-risk people."

"Do you think they'll just throw us in with our clothes on and everything?"

"Becky, this is serious. You *know* what I mean. With Zach about to turn 16, our insurance will soar through the roof. I don't know how you're gonna do it, Honey, but you've *got* to charm your way out of this one. Godspeed."

The first thing that came to mind as I was receiving my marching orders was a bright orange billboard I'd recently seen on the highway. It read: "Traffic Tickets? No problem. Call 1-800-We-Fix-'Em." So I placed a call to a lawyer whose yellow page advertising square looked most like the billboard. The deep male voice on the other end sounded fairly upbeat and hopeful as I described my case...until I told him the name of the judge on the bottom of my ticket.

"Ma'am," he quickly advised, "that's the toughest judge in the county. He doesn't cut anybody any slack once they've missed their court date. Just send 'em the money and pray your insurance company has mercy on you."

I hung up, swallowed hard, and gave myself a pep talk. *Okay, okay. So this judge is no soft touch. And sure, lots of women have tried and failed to cry or sweet-talk their way out of a ticket in his court. But I must not give up. Scott's counting on me; he believes I can do this, and I have to give it my best shot.*

Just then my eyes fell upon a couple of my books and an unfinished manuscript. I turned to a chapter I had recently completed on the subject of my forgetfulness. It was called, "I Never Promised You a Rose Garden. Or Did I? I Can't Seem to Remember."

That's it! I thought, *I'll try to entertain him!*

For the 30 minutes it took me to drive to the county courthouse, I conversed nonstop and fervently with the Almighty.

"God, grant me favor in the eyes of this judge and please, if you see fit, let him be a wanna-be writer." Human nature being what it is, I knew if the judge "had always wanted to write a book," he might very well be putty in my hands.

Upon arrival, I was ushered into the judge's chambers by a secretary in sensible shoes who gave me little in the way of a greeting other than a pitying shake of her head. Sitting down on the edge of a cold vinyl chair in front of an expansive bench, I found myself opposite the "Judge of No Mercy." Nervously, I cleared my throat.

"Your Honor, Sir, first of all, I'd like to explain my situation —"

"Well, you can't," he said without looking up.

"Why not?" I asked, caught more than a little off guard.

"Because first you have to enter a plea. What will it be?"

"Insanity."

With that, he glanced up, and I thought I saw a glimmer of a smile. Perhaps I'd found a soft spot after all. I settled on a more feasible plea of "no load contender"—whatever that is. I told the judge I wanted the one that means, "I'm not saying I did, but I'm not saying I didn't."

This time he definitely smiled. Things were looking up.

I plunged ahead with my plan. I plopped two of my books and the "Forgetful chapter," on top of the mahogany desk between us, and Your Honor's thick eyebrows stood at attention.

Thankfully, I'd dabbled quite a bit in the law—I read two John Grisham novels and viewed *The Firm* on video. Since this meeting occurred during the infamous, televised O.J. trial, I patted the pile and in my best Marsha Clark imitation, I simply said, "Evidence."

Any balanced jury could have seen I was now on an unstoppable roll.

"You see, Your Honor, I'm sure lots of people come in and out of your office every day and *say* they forgot about their traffic tickets. But I have brought you undeniable *proof.* I actually make a living writing about all the things I've forgotten. Short- and long-term memory loss is a handicap, as much as any other physical disability. But you can see from the evidence before you that I've determined to turn my disability into income and inspiration. So when I tell you that I forgot about the ticket in *my* wallet, you can believe beyond any reasonable doubt that I am telling you the truth."

He was quiet for a few seconds. Slowly, he eased his substantial body back into his black leather chair, scratched his chin, and sized me up with a raised brow. I gulped. What had I done now? Whatever it was, it was too late to back out. After what seemed like eons, he broke the silence.

"So you're a writer?"

"Yes, I am. I do so solemnly swear. I mean, I don't swear in my writing. I mean I swear I am a writer. Yes, Your Honor, I do…I mean, I am."

"You know, I've always dreamed of writing a book someday."

Oh, God, You are merciful to me, a forgetter!

From that moment the judge and I were pals, friends— yes, even buds, if you will. He recounted tale after tale of life in a small town courtroom. Before long we were laughing and slapping the bench and having a rousing good time. Then there was a knock at the door. The judge wound down a good story about a little old lady who'd told some amazing whoppers trying to squirm out of a delinquent ticket. Then good-naturedly he called out, "Come on in!"

The gentlemen behind the door peeked in, his face a curious study.

"Thought I ought to check in on you, Judge. Sounds like you're having an awfully good time in here."

"Well, come on in," the judge said amiably. "Got a little gal here I want you to meet. She's real forgetful, so I've been trying to impress upon her the importance of putting out-standing traffic tickets at the top of her priority list. I'd sure hate to see her locked up in your jail."

With that, the judge smiled in my direction and said, "Mrs. Freeman, meet our chief of police."

Turning his attention back to the police chief, the judge spoke with mock sternness, "Listen, this young lady will need a police escort to the city limits. She's real accident prone." Both men broke into a camaraderie of chuckles at my expense. I couldn't have been more thrilled.

As I stood to shake the jovial judge's hand and take my leave, he informed me I could still take the Defensive Driving course to cover my ticket. I floated out of his office on wings of gratitude, but when I told the secretary outside that the judge had granted me mercy, she refused to take my word for it. She wasted no time in picking up the phone and dialing his chambers. A few seconds later, the bewildered woman was staring at the receiver and then at me and back again at the receiver.

"Well, if that don't beat all. What in the world did you say to him?"

I shrugged and replied, "I just told him the facts, Ma'am, just the facts."

Not long after the incident, my mother sent me a greeting card. A Post-It note was attached to the front saying, "You might want to use this the next time you get in a fix with a judge." The front of the card shows a black-and-white photo of an adorable little girl, about five-years-old, wearing a rain slicker and a hat. She's holding an envelope in her out-stretched hand. Her facial expression? Angelic, yet pitiful. Inside, the card reads, "Will you forgive me if I remind you how cute I am?"

Sarah, I have a feeling you and I will need all the "cute" we can get in this life. Though there will be times when others say we are maddening, I hope no one will say we are not entertaining. If we're very good, they might even say we have a certain charm. But just to be on the safe side, I think I'll tape the date for my Defensive Driving course to the dashboard of my vehicle…if I can remember where I put the tape.

Standing in the court, she obtained favor in his sight....

ESTHER 5:2

Charm...it's something we need badly in this mechanized, fragmented, dehumanized world.

Arthur Gordon,
A Touch of Wonder

8

Will You Rub My Back?

Hunger for Touch

It was another one of those over-my-head, insufferably long church services. I was probably four or five years old. I lay my head on my mother's lap and curled my patent leather shoes up under the flounce of my dress. Mother's lap was extra firm this morning, the result of her full-strength Sunday morning girdle. My eyelids grew heavy as she absently stroked my hair and played with one of my curls. I felt loved, cuddled—her baby again. Then came—ahhhh, heaven in a church pew—my mother's fingernails gently etching circles and curlicues and figure eights as they floated up and down my back. Even "Big Church" preaching could be tolerated under the influence of those hypnotic maternal hands.

The soothing power of touch is absolutely amazing.

● ● ●

When I was 13, I contracted hepatitis while on a youth trip. (The form of hepatitis you get from drinking bad water in Mexico, as opposed to the hepatitis you get from doing bad things.)

It was the wee hours of the morning. I couldn't eat, my side ached above a swollen liver, I was weak. I had missed six weeks of school, and now my skin was afire with a rash—a side effect of jaundice. No amount of medicine, baths, or tears would halt the burning itch as it spread from my head to my toes.

My mother, in the early morning darkness, sensed my misery with good old-fashioned mother radar, I suppose. She padded down the hall to my bedroom and here helped me ease from my bed to a clean, comfortable pallet on the living room couch. Then, having done all a mother could do, she began to pray. Her hands rested upon my back, her words pouring quietly into the darkness.

"Father, I come asking relief for my Becky. Please grant her a good night's sleep." After that, all I remember is sliding into sleep with Mother's fingernails gently etching curlicues and circles and figure eights on my back. The insidious itching was miraculously gone. The healing power of prayer, mingled with touch, had worked its wonders.

● ● ●

We read about this powerful God-given force called human touch in psychology and medical studies everywhere. Babies thrive on it, and shrivel up and die without it. (My nine-month-old niece becomes hypnotic with rapture when her skin is stroked with a soft baby brush.) A simple hug has been shown to lower blood pressure and to release feel-happy endorphins. Even stroking a pet is healthy, experts say, because there's something about touching a living, breathing *anything* that breathes life into all that lies hungry under our skin.

A few years ago, Mother and I were interviewed at a local radio station. The host asked Mom for her best advice on raising kids. "Well," she said, "you pray a lot. You laugh often. And you keep touching them. When they're small, rub their backs, stroke their hair. As they become teenagers a quick neck rub or hand on their shoulder may be all they will accept. But don't stop giving your children some measure of physical affection."

My son Gabe, now a teenager and self-conscious of public hugging from Mom, suffers from occasional migraines. One recent episode was so horrible that we took him to the emergency room where doctors performed a CAT scan just to make sure he didn't have a tumor. Nothing would stop the pain, not even an injection of Demerol. Back home in his room, lying in the darkness, I asked if there was anything I might bring him. A cool rag? A drink of water? This man-child could only mumble, "Lie down by me."

So all afternoon, as my son suffered the blinding pain of a migraine, I curled near him, wordless, holding his hand and sometimes rubbing his feet. How I hated to see my child suffer, but I have to admit that I loved the few hours of Gabe being my baby again.

As each of our grandparents took their turn being sick and, eventually, dying, I watched my mother rub their tired feet with warm lotion; caress their weary, wrinkled faces; hold their love-starved hands. She never drew back from physically reaching out to anyone, any age. I love this about her.

We know babies and children must be touched to thrive; I wonder how many adults are suffering from depression and lowered immunity from "caress deprivation"? Studies show that women generally fair better physically and emotionally after a divorce than men. I suspect this is in part because of the snuggles women continue to receive from their children or the hugs they get from their friends when they are hurting. Men who can comfortably say "How about a hug?" or "I need a hug" are few and far between. The few who can live blessed, healthier lives.

Touch is also one of the best ways to express emotions that refuse to be put neatly into words.

A few years ago, I was sitting across from my friend Ruth, sharing a casual lunch of hamburgers, spicy fries, and soft drinks. The setting was average, everyday. Just two women enjoying lunch out at a downtown cafe. Anyone looking at us would have no way of knowing that one of us had experienced the death of her one-year-old son a few days before. Unless passing customers spied a couple of telltale tears slipping down our cheeks and mingling with the ketchup around our mouths, they wouldn't know that Ruth had just suffered a parent's ultimate nightmare. Yet even in the midst of her grief, Ruth managed to occasionally smile and laugh. (And when Ruth laughs, no one can miss it!)

Baby Caleb had been terminally ill since he'd drawn his first breath, so the element of shock was not as strong a factor in Ruth's grief as it might have otherwise been. But grief still comes. Her nursery on this bright morning stood emptied of its precious, smiling, reaching contents. Even so, Ruth, a young woman of boundless courage and determined joy, presses on, looking for the good in all things. Her faith through this season of trial leaves me stunned with admiration. Still I know she aches and I want so much to be of comfort. What can a sister offer another whose world has fallen apart at life's fragile seams?

"Ruth," I ask tentatively, "can you tell me…other than my prayers, what practical things help at a time like this?"

She smiled as she retraced the events of the last few days. "Becky, even though my husband and I knew the end was always one breath away for Caleb, his passing still came as a surprise. I was in a fog all that morning of his death. Friends came with food; the youth group dropped by to clean house, mow the yard, and generally offer their services. All of that helped tremendously. But I still felt so uptight from an anxiousness I could not put my finger on.

"Then a couple of my closest friends sat me down and said, 'Ruth, we want you to think for a second. What do *you* need?' Then out of the blue, I found myself saying, 'I think I need a massage.'"

I laughed. "Had you ever had a massage before?"

"No," she answered, "I don't know why or how I knew what I needed, but God must have known. My friends arranged an appointment that very afternoon with a massage therapist named Adreena. And Becky, it was the strangest thing. It turned out to be exactly what I needed. I lay down on the table, and Adreena began kneading away at the stress and sadness in my weary body. It was *wonderful*. After months of nonstop caring for a critically sick baby, stroking him, tending to his needs, now I was on the receiving end of care. By the time Adreena finished with me an hour later, I found I had the strength to get up and complete the funeral arrangements. My fuzzy head was clear, and I knew I was going to make it through the day. There was something life-affirming about the whole experience."

Ruth's testimony piqued my curiosity. I'd never had a massage. The whole concept of a stranger pouring oil on someone's body and rubbing him or her down seemed a little weird to me. Yet in many other cultures this practice isn't given a second thought.

The author/journalist of *Surviving a Writer's Life*, Suzanne Lipsett, had been emotionally stripped and numbed by a brutal rape and assault in her college years. Seeking any escape from the memories haunting her, she traveled overseas and landed in Istanbul. At one point, she received a massage from an old, wrinkled Turkish woman. Much to her surprise, the mothering, loving touch from the stranger helped turn a corner for Suzanne and her emotional healing.

She wrote, "There was little left in me but gratitude to the woman whose hands had taken time to stroke and knead me. I was clean and warm, a child in the hands of an old, knowing woman whose very body spoke survival of her own nameless ordeals."

In a poignant scene from the movie *At First Sight,* a kindly young blind man named Virgil (played by Val Kilmer) gives a therapeutic massage to a woman caught up in the frantic pace of her life. As he strokes her, she relaxes, seeming to transform on the screen from a know-it-all woman to a helpless child. Then, to her own surprise, she begins to cry from some hidden part of her soul, emotions surfacing as a result of his caring, kneading touch. Virgil affirmed that this happens sometimes because touch can unleash long-buried pain.

I'd heard, read, and seen enough. I decided to call Adreena and experience a massage for myself.

I was worried about disrobing in front of a stranger, even with a towel covering me. I possess several lumps and bulges, not to mention road maps of stretch marks that I prefer to keep under wraps. Then I discovered that Adreena was blind, like the man Val Kilmer portrayed. This put me more at ease. I made an appointment for a Tuesday afternoon.

Adreena turned out to be a pretty black woman in her early sixties. She wore a simple cotton dress with her hair pulled up in a bun. When I walked into the room, she greeted me in a lilting voice.

"Well, hello! I'm over here, Hon, be with you in a second."

I undressed and lay down on the table, covered only by a towel, and growing uneasier about this idea as the seconds ticked by. I told myself this was just an experiment; I would be like a reporter on assignment. Adreena walked into the room, turned the radio to an easy-listening station, poured lotion on her hands and started in on my neck.

Whoa. I was instant putty. A lump of dough. *Yes*, I thought, *I can probably handle this assignment after all.*

While Adreena kneaded my muscles, I started a conversation. I began by telling her how much she had meant to my friend Ruth on a painful, heart-wrenching day.

"Ruth?" Adreena asked enthusiastically. "Oh, Honey, I liked her right away. She told me she'd just lost her baby boy. What can you say to a mother at a time like that? I just tried to love and comfort her through my hands. I believe my abilities are a gift, and every day I pray that God will use me to minister love."

"Adreena," I mumbled as my body unwound in places I never even knew were tense, "what made you decide to do this for a living?"

"Well," she began, turning around to gather more lotion, "I like people. One good thing about being blind is that I honestly never think about a person's color. Their looks don't matter to me at all—it's their personalities and voices I remember.

"Also, I knew I'd be good at this because I sincerely care about people. I've had massages, and I can tell the ones that are given with a sense of caring and the ones that are given out of duty. Without sight, all your other senses grow stronger, so I can tell a lot about people from something as simple as touch."

I closed my eyes and listened as Adreena went on to tell me how, as a little girl, she's lost her sight after a series of operations for a brain tumor. She told of a mother who had wanted the best for her and, even though life was hard, had found a way to send Adreena to one of the best schools for the blind in the country.

Adreena's inspiration was infectious as she continued talking and kneading.

"You got to have faith in God and in yourself. Set realistic goals. When we do something we're a little afraid of—but we believe in ourselves and have faith and get it done—it strengthens us. My mother and my teacher and my friends at the blind school all taught me these things. I'm here to tell you they work! I finally believed in myself, and I've never been afraid to venture out."

While Adreena massaged my shoulders, arms, and hands—even the grooves between my fingers—I discovered more about her life. She had once been married and now had two grown daughters. She spoke with her grown children almost daily, she said, but she's quite content to live alone. She talked of the exciting occasion when as a teenager she'd taken her first plane trip, a trip to get her first seeing-eye dog, a collie shepherd named Susan. When Susan died after 14 years of faithful companionship, it had been like losing a member of the family. Her children were heartbroken as well. Adreena never replaced Susan. She said she just never saw the need to.

"Do you ever get depressed, Adreena?" I asked lazily, curious to know if this lively woman ever suffered moments of despair.

"Now, I'm not Superwoman or anything," she answered as she continued working away with her magic fingers. "Sometimes I get down in the dumps, and then I have me a good cry. Then I say, 'Lord I don't want to feel this way.' I hate those times. It's like an artery is plugged up in my spirit. I can't give out all the love and joy I want to be giving. Every Sunday morning it's my job to give an inspirational statement at my church. The congregation just seems to love it, but I love it even more. I've got so much inspiration coming my way now, with people handing me quotes and verses and such, that I had to ask them to let me give two every Sunday."

Adreena rubbed my feet with a circular motion and applied long firm strokes to the backs of my ankles. I was melting.

I vowed to teach my husband how to do this.

"Adreena?"

"Yes."

"Why don't you go ahead and give me the full treatment. Inspire me with one of your favorite sayings."

"Well, all right. Here's one of my favorites." She slowed down for effect, "With God's arms under us and His love around us we can face anything before us."

"Oooh, that's a good one." I turned over like a chicken on a spit to get the other side done.

"How's 'bout this?" Adreena paused from her work a moment, adopting her Sunday morning voice. "Earth's worst often turns out to be heaven's best."

"Your church must be awfully proud to have you there," I commented. "Adreena, may I ask you one more question?"

"Sure."

"If you had to choose between being blind or deaf, which would you choose?"

Adreena's response was surprisingly enthusiastic. "I believe I would have to choose to be blind because there's too many things I love to hear. I *love* music. Oh, how I love music! And the birds! How could I stand it if I couldn't hear the birds? I hear them sing, and I'm so thankful for their cheerful voices in the morning. And the sound of a baby's coo, and the little noise my dog made when she'd hand me her paw or lay her head on my lap! And the voices of my children. No, I can't even imagine not being able to hear!"

The thought of her children and grandchildren led Adreena to one last piece of advice before she ended my "therapy" session.

"And about children. Hon, you have to *listen* to children. They want to tell you things you may not think are very important, but if you really listen to them because it's important to *them*, oh my, how children need that. I used to read books, from Braille, to my children. They *loved* that attention. And when they were babies I nursed them because I knew the closeness was good for them. Now my daughters want to do the same with their babies."

"Adreena," I observed, "because of your blindness I'm sure out of pure necessity your children had more physical contact with you than most children have with their mothers. Maybe that's one of the many reasons you have such great relationships with them."

She nodded and smiled as I rolled off the table, limp as a rag, refreshed and renewed.

Driving home, feeling almost boneless, I began to recall all the times Jesus used touch as a tool for physical and emotional healing: a withered hand was made whole by His touch; a blind man saw his family and friends for the first time after the Master touched his eyes. The beloved disciple John leaned on Jesus in the same way he'd seen dozens of children relax into the Savior's embrace. Crowds pressed in just to touch the hem of Christ's garment, and they received many miracles for their trouble. A woman of questionable repute washed Jesus' feet with her tears, wiping them with her hair. Though others were taken aback by this emotional intensity—by her open display of intimate caring through touch—Jesus never flinched. In fact, He gave her the highest praise.

As one of His last acts on earth, Jesus held the feet of His friends in His own two hands, washing and massaging away the dirt and dust of the world they walked in.

And today He tells us to go and do likewise.

He is always reminding us to reach out and touch someone else—and to allow them to touch us as well. Someday God Himself promises to personally wipe the tears away from every eye. But while we are bound in earth-time, God does not physically stroke our human skin or embrace us with a presence we can feel tactilely. That's why He made us of bone and soft flesh and trusted us with the cherished, temporary duty of being His hands to each other.

Jesus came and touched them....

MATTHEW 17:7

9

All by Myself

Gaining Healthy Independence

he French writer, Collette, hit the nail on the head when she wrote, "There are days when solitude is a heady wine that intoxicates you with freedom."

One of the things I most looked forward to as a child was someday getting to Grown-up Land because then, I knew I'd finally get to do stuff *all by myself.*

This old daydream of mine is leading up to a small confession: I'm feeding a childish indulgence on a regular basis—acting out, I suppose, the desire to prove I can do whatever I want to do, whenever I want to do it, and do it all by myself, thank you very much. At least in one small area of my life. I have to admit that nearly every day of my adult life I stop by a convenience store to buy myself a little "treat"—a cola or one of those interesting bottled teas, a piece of pizza, an egg roll, a box of Junior Mints, or some such delicacy. Or if I'm on a diet (which averages about every third day), I'll buy bottled water or a cup of coffee and simply sniff or gaze longingly in the direction of the candy bar aisle. Most often I wind up purchasing nonsensical fluff, completely void of nutritional, educational, or spiritual value. Though it is thoroughly politically and nutritionally incorrect, I confess that I adore these goody-seeking jaunts. I look forward to them as much as a nap in a hammock or 30 minutes alone with a good book.

I know, I know. It's probably a power issue fraught with myriad dangerous physiological, not to mention, psychological implications. Yet from earliest childhood, I've dreamed of the day I could be on my own, driving my own car, carrying my own coins, and buying my own treats sans the hassle of begging or pleading or finagling my parents. I'd fantasize of marching headlong into the corner store any old time I pleased, relishing the control I could wield over my own destiny. Would it be a soft drink, a snack cake, a candy bar, or an ice cream today?

When I get to be a grown-up, I'd think with abandoned glee, *why, I can go to the store* all by myself! *Without asking a single adult for permission or loose change!* This is one of my few childhood fantasies that have actually panned out to my expectations! Of course, my requirements for what qualifies as excitement are admittedly low, but everyday I look forward to declaring and living out this tiny bit of independence.

And if I have my druthers, I prefer my local out-in-the-sticks convenience stores: Big Daddy's, The Village Bait & Tackle Store, Get-It-Kwik. They are filled with the aroma of stale smoke and their offerings often consist of petrified edibles and RC colas with aluminum lids doubling as dust catchers, but I get a kick out of these hometown Mom-and-Pop operations.

Why? Because I can walk into any one of these places with my baggy purple shorts, my old red "Go Lone Oak Buffalos" T-shirt, my hair pulled up with those squeegee contraptions, bare feet, no make-up—I can always rest assured that there will be someone in the store who looks even worse than me. All in all, I believe this ritual to be a relatively harmless addiction.

It is extremely important, of course, that I get away for my excursion *all by myself*. I'm really sneaky when the kids are home and it's time to head out, *solo*, for my treat fix. I've even been known to put the car in neutral and let it slide backwards out of the driveway so as not to alert the troops I'm about to escape for a few moments of respite. If I don't, they start running out of the house like orphaned children stranded on a desert island, begging—as if for their life—to "go with." I used to relent and take them, but after umpteen fights over "he gets more stuff than me" and 20 dollars down the drain trying to even it all out, I realized one day I was *not* having fun anymore. So these days I make my get-away quickly and quietly.

Besides, I soothe my conscience, *my kids will have to wait their own turns to be grown-ups and buy junk food whenever they want. I had to wait all my childhood for this coveted reward, so can they.*

When Zach had been driving for nearly a month, I was truly enjoying watching him discover the joy and privileges of semi-adulthood. It's been surprising to discover how beneficial it is to have an extra driver around the house. Most obviously, Zach no longer begged and prodded me to take him to from point A to points B through Z and back again. He can get there in his own car *all by himself*. Not only does he take care of his own transportation, but also his snacks, his entertainment, and—more and more—his general all-over life.

Which means I get more luxurious time to spend *all by myself!*

My mother phoned the other day to ask me about her eldest grandson's newfound independence. Mom's got a new car phone, and I can always tell when she is using it because she's convinced herself she must shout in order to be heard way out there on the highway—seeing as how the cellular phone's so far from her telephone lines and all. She cannot believe the small receiver actually works. It looks too much like a dime store toy, she declares.

Anyway, via the satellite airwaves, I could hear Mother's hollering loud and clear. *"So, Sister, how are you handling your oldest son driving a car?"* (Mother always calls me "Sister" whenever she talks to me on the telephone. I have no idea why. I think it's a generic name system, a holdover from her West Texas roots where everyone coming in and out of the house was a sister or brother to somebody.)

"Mother," I answered in a voice I knew bordered on that of a preschool teacher's, "let's try to talk just a little more softly, please. I promise that toy phone of yours works really, really well....I am *thrilled* that Zach's driving. This is one time in my life when my forgetful nature has been a real boon. I keep forgetting when Zach is gone, when he is supposed to be home, and what time I'm supposed to start worrying. The other night, I didn't even know he'd gone out so I was taken completely off guard when Zach walked in the front door and apologized all over himself for being an hour late. Because I didn't want him to think I'm not a conscientious mother, I scolded, 'Son, you had me worried sick! What's the matter? You didn't have a quarter to call home?' I really should have added, 'Next time pick up the phone and let me know when you aren't in your bedroom!'"

Mother laughed so loud I thought my eardrum would burst. *"Well, Honey, this may be a big load off your shoulders, to have Zach with wheels and all!"*

"Mother, I love you. But if you don't tone down that volume I'm going to have to put you—I mean *the phone*—down on the floor."

"Oops. I forgot. I just can't believe..."

"That little toy phone works so well. I know. But trust me, it does. Like a charm. Now back to Zach. My life has simplified overnight since Zachary got his own car. You know how he's always been chomping at the bit to do his own thing? With his new freedom, our relationship has really relaxed and improved. I only wish I'd thought about getting him a driver's license when he was two!"

Our conversation wound down, but I can't say the same for the volume. After yelling goodbye (if you can't beat 'em, join 'em), I hung up massaging my right ear as I walked from the bedroom to the kitchen. I couldn't help pondering the "all by myself" experiences that mark our children's lives as they move from childhood into adulthood.

One day a newborn arrives into our arms. So helpless and needy. In the space of a few months, our baby is holding a bottle or cup—all by himself. The next thing we parents know, our once-helpless infant is crawling, toddling, breaking eggs, and pouring milk into cracks in the floor—all by himself. Then comes the tearful day our pint-sized son insists upon walking into a brick building and down the hall into a school classroom—all by himself. And some teacher forever takes over our position as "primary daytime adult companion."

Other solo rites of passage come so quickly the rest of childhood flies by in a blur. They learn to ride bikes—alone. There's the milestone of listening to our children insist they can go into the doctor's examining room—unattended by mom. Next, they're driving cars by themselves and going out on dates without chaperones. Then, hopefully, they'll find and hold down a job—all by themselves. All by themselves, one day, our kids will choose mates, set up housekeeping, and begin having babies of their own. Babies who, in the span of a few short months, will be holding their own bottles—all by themselves.

● ● ●

Today I'm marveling at how many more "firsts" my children have hit. Zach has made me a grandmother, Zeke has been married to Amy for more than a year, and Rachel is planning to get married to her sweetheart, Jody. Gabe is a freshman in high school, so I'll have a bit of kid company for the next four years, but I know when Gabe turns 16 and gets his own set of wheels he'll be as excited to be free to cruise around town all by himself as I was at his age. (What am I saying? I am *still* excited to be cruising around town all by myself.)

Sometimes I even miss the days when all the kids were underfoot, and I had to sneak out of the driveway for time alone. If I do ask if anyone wants to "go with," the answer is most often, "No thanks, Mom. I'm really busy."

But I remind myself that their growing desire for independence is not about their losing their love for me. It's about them growing up to be comfortable with others, and equally as comfortable being all by themselves. Was it Carl Jung who said most of our problems come from the inability to be alone with ourselves in a room?

When I was a first-grade teacher (before I retired from my nine long months of faithful service), I wrote a little children's book about moments when we need, and indeed, want to be alone. My class full of kids loved it! (I saw one of my little first-grade students today. He is playing varsity football. I am old.) Without benefit of my lovely, homemade, finger-painted illustrations, I will describe the pertinent scenes as I share my "book."

All by Myself

Sometimes when I am happy
and want to sing and dance
I'll find a place
A quiet place
To hide
All by Myself

I sing, I twirl
I put on a show—
Where no one else
But me, will know

*(Scene of a tree house and a
little girl dancing and kicking up her heels)*

Sometimes when I'm upset
And want to cry or scream
I'll find a place
A quiet place
To hide
All by Myself

I'll fuss, I'll stomp
I'll SHOUT, SHOUT, SHOUT!
Until The Mad is all yelled out.

*(Scene by trees and a pond,
little girl having a royal fit)*

Sometimes when I feel crowded
and want to get away

*(Little girl surrounded and squished
by numerous siblings)*

I'll find a place

A quiet place
To hide
All by Myself

(Little girl in bathtub,
pink bubbles everywhere)

I hop in the tub
And scoot down low
And pop the bubbles
With my toe.
Sometimes when I am tired
And want to fall asleep

(girl is yawning)

I'll find a place
A quiet place
To hide
All by Myself
Then snuggle deep
Inside my bed
My pillow sinks
Beneath my head

(Pigtailed little girl sitting on a windowseat,
contentedly looking out at the world)

I like Myself
I'm nice to know
So with Myself
I like to go
Sometimes you see
I like to be
All by myself
With only me*

10

I Can't Wait 'til Camp!

Peer-Bonding in the Great Outdoors

Each summer in East Texas, I drive my car through a set of iron gates (thankfully, they usually are open) and cruise down an oil-topped road. One time just as I was rounding a certain curve, I encountered a large animal. The beast planted itself in the middle of the road, and there it stood, methodically chewing its cud like a contented old man with a juicy plug of tobacco. Having grown accustomed to life outside the big city, the first time this happened I wasn't all that shocked to come upon a huge, cud-chewing animal sunning itself in the center of traffic. But this was no bovine! For one, this creature had a hump on its back. And its legs rose to the top of my vehicle. Yes, it was a camel—of the Arabian desert variety.

The dromedary began eyeing my hood ornament hungrily and licking his chops in anticipation. Not knowing what to do, I honked the horn. All I got in response was the nonchalant blink of his ebony eyes. He would not move.

What? Had I thought he could be honked into action like some common Hereford or Jersey?

Just then a long-legged cowboy strode by and tossed out some advice.

"I'd go around him if I were you. He's fixing to spit."

And so I did. Speedily in fact, and—may I add—none too soon.

Welcome to Jan-Kay Ranch, Detroit, Texas.

I came to this unusual setting to bring my daughter, Rachel, and her two girlfriends for a week of summer camp. Little brother, Gabe, also tagged along for the ride. But when he saw the camel, and then the llamas, antelopes, wild pigs, peacocks, monkeys, and, of course, the tiger, bear, and baby elephant—it was all too much. How dare I bring him this close to paradise only to take him home again!

What does a good, sensible mother do in such situations? I haven't the foggiest. I only know that this mother ended up leaving her son at camp with a plastic Wal-Mart bag full of clothes scrounged from the recesses of her station wagon.

Honestly, I knew Gabe would be fine at this family owned camp. I knew it because years before I went to this very same ranch with the junior high group from my church. The wild and exotic animals weren't around back then, but the cabins and rec hall and lake were exactly as I remembered them.

● ● ●

I had loved those church camp weeks at Jan-Kay Ranch. I enjoyed watching the early morning mist rise over the lake as whitewashed egrets flew from stump to fish and back again. My first clear memories of spiritual stirrings happened at that camp, as Scripture began to make sense. I found, lying between the covers of the Bible, fascinating situations involving what I now call "Camelots of the Soul"—stories where truth and goodness and mercy and right stood their ground in the midst of cruelty and jealousy and confusion and wrong. It was refreshing. As a teenager, I found myself especially hungry for such shining visions. (One doesn't find many shining visions in the daily halls of public school.)

I also remember the beating of my heart as I stepped out of my cabin on summer evenings, just-showered and sweet-smelling after a day filled with team games and noise and sweat. I can almost hear the screen door bouncing behind me with its rhythmic squeak and feel the adolescent hoping-beyond-hope that a cute boy might walk by the porch, take notice, and smile in my direction. Evening hayrides. Midnight gossip. Afternoon swims. Morning walks.

Nice memories. Very nice.

● ● ●

Some time ago, I was invited back to Jan-Kay Ranch to attend a women's retreat. I rediscovered the mist and the lake, unchanged and serene. On this stay there would be no boys to impress, however. The boys had turned into husbands—*our husbands*—who were staying home with our children so we could escape them all for a weekend. And we women had come hoping to rediscover a bit of spiritual Camelot in the midst of our hectic, modern lives. Along with absorbing the Scriptures for its goodness and truth, we also played and yakked and laughed and ate goodies till the wee hours. To get to Camelot, m'lady, there needs be some fun along the way.

I believe every woman should have a chance to go back to camp again. For one thing, it's great on the ego to see other gorgeous, sophisticated women without their make-up, and dressed in flannel, feet pajamas. It has a way of bringing high-church ladies down to my comfort level. With the make-up removed, masks also dropped with more ease, and the resulting gab sessions were the best. I, for one, didn't want to miss out on any late-night, impromptu round circles.

One night during the retreat, way past midnight, I was plagued with bunkbed insomnia. Feeling slumber-partyish anyway, I climbed down from my perch and pulled a plate of brownies from my food stash. I was a woman on a mission. Fairly confidant I could find another night owl, somewhere, I walked out into the darkness seeking some friend with whom I could share a chocolate conversation.

Without my contact lenses, it was a terrific challenge to feel my way through the blackness. But finally I spotted a lone figure sitting on the front porch in the moonlight. I walked toward the woman, sat down beside her, looked up at the starry night, and said dreamily, "Isn't it beautiful out here? I guess you couldn't sleep either, huh? Listen—I come bearing gifts. Would you like a fudge brownie?"

There was no answer. The woman sat stone still, staring straight ahead.

Oh, great, I thought, *she must have wanted to be alone.*

But as I looked closer, I jumped back with a start. The figure was not a woman after all. I'd just offered my brownies to a wooden Indian!

As I rose to find more lively companionship, I patted the Indian's knee and offered him some free advice, "Fella, you really should loosen up." The incident was a big hit when I finally found a live, nocturnal audience to share my brownies and my story.

● ● ●

As much fun as it is to fellowship, there *is one big drawback* to camp, of which you should be forewarned: All camp directors seem to insist on organizing some form of physical group activity. It conjures images of that ugly childhood word: "P.E." I didn't like it when I was 12, and I don't like it any better now. After what happened at one retreat I attended, I like it even less than you can imagine. But, still, I know it's good for my character to be stretched beyond my comfort zone every once in a while.

The fateful physical activity to which I'm referring had ominous overtones from the start. The idea was for us ladies to participate in what is called a Ropes Course. If you've never heard of them, they are a series of challenges involving wood and ropes and needlessly frightening tests designed to help bond a team together (from sheer terror, I assume).

The nightmare of tests is the Trust Fall. At this juncture in the course, we were to ascend a platform some four feet in height. Then we, being adults of sane mind, were to fall backwards—one at a time—from that height into the locked and waiting hands of our fellow middle-aged, baggy-armed comrades. I learned one thing from that experience. Peer pressure doesn't ever completely loosen its grip; even in midlife. To chants of, "Don't be a sissy, Becky," I climbed, I fell, they caught, and it hurt like the dickens.

When it was my turn to join the "catchers," I was relieved. "Better to be a catcher than the fall guy," I always say. The next woman to climb the platform was rather large. When she plummeted, we did our best to break her fall, but down to the ground she went with a sickening thud. Stunned, the fallen woman shook her head as if to clear it. Then she uttered the bravest words ever spoken by a mere mortal.

"I want to try it again," she said.

I could not believe it. We'd just dropped this woman, our friend, on a Trust Fall, for goodness sake. Hadn't we just proven we were not the sorts to be trusted?

But she believed in us, and she believed in herself. As our fearless faller began her climb, I locked arms with a woman named Gracie who stood across from me. She whispered to me under her breath, "Becky, if you let go, I'll kill you. We have to make this catch."

Our Lady of Bravery, ready for her descent, stood on the platform and turned slowly around. She fell straight back, arms folded across her chest. *We caught her!* (Hallelujah!) Boy, it hurt like the dickens, but the whole experience resulted in a new hero added to my personal vision of Camelot. In my eyes, this brave woman became a true knight in shining armor. She was determined to see our ragtag group rise to the challenge and, even though we failed her once, she was willing to sacrifice her own body, King Arthur style, so our faith in each other—and in all humankind—could be restored.

(It also proved to be a remarkable bonding experience. Because I did not let go, Gracie didn't kill me. In fact, that afternoon was the start of a remarkable friendship, and after nearly a decade of lunching, writing, tears, and laughter, Gracie and I are still hanging on like crazy to each other.)

Having learned such a significant moral lesson, I limped back to my cabin, warm with emotion. I had forced myself to experience the ultimate camp challenge, been part and parcel of a team's success, and I had to admit it was a good feeling. Wild horses couldn't drag me into doing a Ropes Course again, or I am now officially at the "End of my ropes"—but I'm proud to say, "I did it!"

● ● ●

Yes, these are the types of experiences that make an unforgettable week of camp: conquering challenges, teamwork, beautiful scenery, nature's animals, late-night talks, spiritual refreshment, and chocolate. Mulling it over, I knew that Gabe, my youngest adventurous son, would be a natural for summer camp—even with nothing but a plastic bag full of old clothes. As it turned out, I couldn't have been more correct.

I made a midweek visit to Jan-Kay, carrying fresh clothing rations for my little camper-to-go. Once I made it past the camel guard, and parked my car, hood ornament intact, it didn't take long to locate Gabe. He was happily feeding Eedie the baby elephant fistfuls of popcorn. As I strolled up to say hello, I saw Eedie stretch out her trunk, grab the popcorn bag Gabe was holding and, in an instant, gulp it down paper and all.

Gabe was startled at first, and then he got tickled as only little kids can—breaking out in a gale of spontaneous giggles. The scene of Gabe bent over with laughter, and the elephant scarfing down his bag of popcorn went "click" in that place in my head where pictures I don't want to forget are stored. *At moments like this Gabe makes it look like so much fun to be a kid. And if I can't be one, at least it's awfully fun to have one.*

Though he looked as happy as I've ever seen him, I wondered if my baby had suffered any routine gone-away-to-camp-for-the-first-time homesickness. I'd been reading Art Linkletter's latest edition of *Kids Say the Darndest Things* and had come across a letter written by one little homesick soul trying to keep up a brave-camper front. It read,

> Dear Mom and Dad, I am not homesick. Please write to me. Are you coming Sunday? Please come. I need some clean towels. Write and tell me if you are coming. Please come and bring the baby. They keep us so busy here I don't have time to get homesick. Please come Sunday. Love, Paul. P.S. Next year I think I'll come to camp for the shorter period.

After reading Paul's pitiful letter, I wanted to be especially sensitive to my son in this, his first extended experience away from home.

"Gabe," I asked gingerly, "have you had any crying spells? At night maybe?"

"Yeah," he answered sheepishly, "last night I did."

I nodded sympathetically and rubbed his back. He continued, a twinge of bittersweet to his voice.

"I cried because camp only lasts for three more days, and I want to stay forever."

That did it. I was convinced. Every kid should get a chance to at least try a wonderful, healthy, eye-opening camp experience. Especially kids like you and me, who still need to commune with nature, laugh out loud in surprise, have our faith refreshed, and establish deeper friendships. Kids who are, forever and always, in search of whatever bits of Camelot can be found in this hard-edged, ol' world.

He satisfies me with good things and makes me young again.

PSALM 103:5 NCV

11

Can't We
Stay a Little Longer?

Love of Play Time

I am bummed. I mean *really* bummed out. I just got home from summer vacation, you see, and I'm not quite ready for life. It's like I found the most perfect, peaceful place to hide; then just as I settled into a calm "ahhh..." big, clumsy ol' Real Life shouts, "Ready or not, here I come!" And within seconds, I am discovered and hauled by the scruff of my neck back into the game.

● ● ●

This morning life forced me up early and into a game of "Follow the Kids to the Station Wagon." Upon my offspring's arrival at the car doors, all four of them broke out in a rousing chorus of "I Get the Front Seat." The participants then began to battle each other in what looked like a wild game of Twister; they were all tangled up trying to reach the coveted seat of honor. At that point I changed the game to "Let's Make a Deal," claimed "Monopoly" on the front seat, and refused to move until all children were ready to participate in "Sorry." (Okay, enough of the game motif.)

After finally depositing the children at school, I drove back home—and it was then I realized the horrible truth. Today, all by myself, I'd have to *clean* the whole entire *yucky* house; *cook* supper (from scratch, mind you), and then make wild after-school *zig-zags* all over town picking up my *umpteen* kids from every conceivable form of "practice." Not only that but I'd also have to sit down and *work*, which means actually *using my brain* to make sense of the little black marks floating across the computer screen at the tap of my fingers. Am I sounding just a wee bit cranky? Forgive me, but sometimes I get so frustrated. Will you indulge me just a second longer?

Right now, what really rots my sandals is that waiting to greet me on my office desk is IRS Form 1040A—the incredibly, unbelievably looooong version, along with all of its tricky little friends: 8898, 4562, and Schedules A through Z. (Yes, I should have filed them in April, but I always ask for an extension. Never do today what you can put off for four months, I always say.) As a result I'm cross-eyed and bewildered and, yes, even paranoid. I just know there is an IRS agent with beady little eyes and an evil sense of humor sitting in some government office waiting for me to misplace a decimal. (Um, just in case an IRS agent is reading this—I'm just teasing with the "beady little eyes, evil sense of humor" bit. But according to line 42, section b, page 55-A, I believe "teasing about the IRS" is "allowable.")

I want you to know that all of this nonproductive whining does have a point. It's…*now what was it?* Oh, yes. The transition from Play Time to Clean-Up Time is the pits. I hated it in kindergarten, and I don't like it any better as an adult. Visualize a toddler wailing—one of those open-mouthed out-loud whines, and you'll have a perfect picture of how I feel right now.

I don't wanna come home yet!! I'll do my chores next month! I wanna go back and PLAY some more!! WAAAAAH!

But maybe (sniff, sniff) if I could tell you how much fun I had on my summer vacation (pitiful swallow), and about the good time I had with my friends, maybe I'll feel all better again.

My Summer Vacation
by Becky Freeman

First and foremost, I've got to tell you about the great big ocean.

I could sit for hours near the sea, just watching her emerald waves toss up soft foam toward sandy shores then pull it all back out again, as if reluctant to hand over such lacy treasure. Show and tell, take it back, then show and tell again.

The beach is also a rather noisy place. Yet the crashing of the waves is another thing I love about retreating to the sea. I don't believe people usually come to the ocean to sort through complicated problems. The din of sloshing seawater assures active thinking will be kept to a minimum, at best.

I believe, instead, that people come to the ocean to be swept away, to let the whooshing, repetitive sound of the pounding waves wash out tired, muddled heads. The laborious swooooosh...swooooosh...leaves you empty, limp, and clean. Like a head massage...or a mental rinse. I guess you could say it's a lovely experience in brainwashing. And the sheer gift of a nonthinking day spent watching the gentle tug-of-war between sea and shore, and of listening to the white noise of the playful struggle, well, *that's* only the *beginning*.

Because it is at night, after the sun makes its crimson bow, that glitter comes out for display. On this particular trip, a full moon dropped by for a welcomed visit. I'd never seen a full moon over the ocean at night, and I almost ached with the beauty of the scene. Luminescent, with its eye wide open, hovering over the dark velvet waves like something wise, gentle, maternal. In response to the glowing roundness in the sky, thousands of diamond lights danced their gratitude from the crests of rolling seawater.

Walking over a dune that night, unprepared as I was for the gorgeous panorama rising before my eyes, I understood the old expression "it takes my breath away." When I found my breath, I whispered quiet praise to the Artist of the masterpiece.

(Isn't this a good vacation story so far? My brow is already beginning to unfurrow. This is very therapeutic. Thank you.)

Are you wondering, "Just exactly what did you do on vacation besides participate in poetic waxing?" Okay, okay, I'm getting to that.

I did absolutely anything I wanted to do at any given moment! For days. Six of them to be exact.

Actually, I did do *some* things. I made our bed once or twice, but I confess that I enjoyed it. Even housework can be fun in tasteful surroundings belonging to wealthy, yuppie-condo-landlords. The furniture in our bedroom was white wicker, the walls pale green, and the bedspread thick and covered with fat pink roses. And there was a lovely balcony where I could slip out at anytime to rest between the exertion of fluffing pillows and tucking in coverlets.

I also did a little cooking—toast, salad, and cold cereal to be exact. A few times I managed to whip up some real meals. There are witnesses that can testify that I also made chilidogs, Bisquick biscuits, and coleslaw from a mix. Somehow we managed to stay happily nourished.

One of the best parts of our annual vacation is that we usually go with friends. This year we went with two couples: Ron and Gail, Dean and Heather...and their children. Luckily, Gail cooks rich treats like pecan brownies and sour cream coffee cake *from scratch*. And Heather, well, Heather knows how to both buy *and* boil shrimp. And because she's got just the right touch of obsessive/compulsiveness, the kitchen stays spotless. Culinary matters aren't of much consequence anyway, since eating out at oceanside cafes has become our group's favorite all-weather water sport.

When vacationing with others, we've found it's important to have similar likes and dislikes. For example, Gail and I are always on a budget, which we don't like. But then there's shopping, which we do like. Very much. Luckily for determined bargain hunters like Gail and me (with little to no sense of pride), there's always a way to get our shopping fix. You should see the great stuff we've picked up from resale shops, Goodwill, and Salvation Army stores along the coastal highways!

One of our "finds" on this trip was a used bookstore. This particular bookstore was in a converted upstairs apartment. It seemed odd that the young proprietor was wearing a tie with his shirt, but he had recently retired from military service. He greeted us warmly and apologized for the mess, not knowing how really low our standards of neatness are. Since I read at least five books during vacation week, I love browsing for reading treasure, especially something that will touch my heart or lift my spirit. In the stacks of dusty books lining the floors and shelves, I found a couple of pearls: a 50-year-old copy of *The Robe* by Lloyd C. Douglas and a 30-year-old copy of *Gifts from the Sea* by Anne Morrow Lindbergh.

When it was time to pay for our books, the shopkeeper surprised us with a serendipitous method for determining the price. Flashing a smile, he asked, "Do you know the game 'Paper, Rock, Scissors'?" Puzzled, we nodded. "Well, here's the deal. If you win you can name the price. But if I win, I get to set the price. Fair enough?"

We were game. Why not? Unfortunately, Bookstore Man won. I held my breath, waiting to hear his price.

"How's two dollars sound?" he asked.

For two hardback books? Are you kidding? I thought. He charged Gail an entire $1.50 for her small stack.

As we turned to leave with our bargains, already tickled with our good fortune, our young man pulled fresh flowers from a nearby vase and handed each of us one as a parting gift. We felt like schoolgirls.

A surprising number of the people we met in Florida went out of their way to be pleasant. Maybe it's the climate. Maybe it's the simple way of life; shorts and sandals are standard attire in even the finest of restaurants. Perhaps it's just that people in Florida stay in an eternally pleasant state of mind. We even came upon a nearby town called Niceville. *Niceville?* Gail and I had to check it out. We found a native Nicevillian working behind a convenience store counter and plied him with all sorts of questions.

"Are people *really* nice here? Is there always a breeze? Do you ever see mosquitoes? What are the schools like? How's the crime rate? Do you just *love* living here?"

I never thought I'd ever consider moving from our East Texas home, but I was tempted for the first time in years to pull up anchor and move to the oceanside.

If Gail keeps me company on shopping sprees, then Heather's my comrade in devouring books and also in the quest to know the answer to everything there is to know about everything—especially the "true meaning of life." One night, the rest of the clan went out for a while, leaving us bookworms alone in the living room. But as soon as the door slammed shut, Heather sat up with a start, put her book down, and fired her opening sentence.

"Okay, Becky, let's catch up!"

And we were off! At the end of an hour, we'd only hit the tip of our theological/ philosophical icebergs. But just as we were getting warmed up, kids of all ages began pouring through the front door anxious to share their latest adventure and our time was gone.

Yes, it was a good vacation. Good friends, good conversation, good shopping, good food, great schedule.

And this year we also had lots of teenagers among the children in our group—Zach, Zeke, and Rachel; Dean and Heather's 19-year-old Jarin; and Ron and Gail's girls, Mandie-Lee, Laressa, and their friend, Amy. I must admit that much of my luxurious sense of freedom was due in part to the fact that my children are entering a wonderful stage of independence. Those long years of having to be constantly on the lookout for little ones is fast coming to a close. (A wonderful consolation prize for that pregnancy test I mentioned at the outset of this book.)

Our teens were amazingly uncomplaining, polite, fun, and just plain good this year if I do say so myself. After watching them together this summer, I'm convinced they'll be friends for life, just as their parents have been all these years.

As an added bonus, a couple of our teenagers now drive. However, the only vehicle that would hold them all for their short excursions about town was poor old Sag. One year, within three hours of the resort, Sag suddenly expired on the highway. But after about ten minutes of rest, he gathered up the strength to start his engine again and moseyed on down the highway for another hour, whereupon he felt the need for another roadside break. At the time, none of Sag's weary contents found this amusing. But a couple of days after we'd said our goodbyes to the beach and unpacked our bags in Texas, I found a letter in the mailbox addressed to "Sag & Those Within." It read,

Dear Sag, we wrote this in your honor. Thanks for the memories.

Sag, the Tragic Wagon
Traveled to the sea
And weaved all over I–20
As far as we could see
Sag, the Tragic Wagon
Had traveled there before
But previously had to stop and rest
Every hour and sometimes more!

Sag, the Tragic Wagon
Had many squished in the back
Including one lonely watermelon,
Gabe, Rachel, Zeke, and Zach!

Love,
Mandie-Lee, Laressa, and Amy

I wonder if people who may be thinking about checking into a mental hospital ought to try six days of doing nothing at the beach first. It would be much less expensive over the long haul and a lot more fun! And, if you're still nuts at the end of six days, the mental ward will always be ready.

Since you've helped me unburden myself today (Bless you!), please feel free to drop by in about 25 years for chili-dogs, Bisquick biscuits, and coleslaw. You'll find us listed in the Niceville directory.

*Don't underestimate the value
of Doing Nothing, of just
going along, listening to
all the things you can't hear,
and not bothering.*

Winnie-the-Pooh

**Come to me, all you who are weary and
burdened, and I will give you rest.**

MATTHEW 11:28

12

I Don't Wanna Go to Church!

Heart-to-Heart Chats with God

W hat is it? What's wrong with me?"

I set my cup down on the coffeeshop table as I rested the side of my face on the palm of my hand. As long as I was in this far, I went ahead and unleashed the rest of it.

"I can't stand church."

It was a childish statement—exaggerated, to be sure— but it welled up within me in a candid, unguarded moment and spilled out into the atmosphere. And there my confession hung for a few seconds, suspended like a soap bubble before it bursts. My three friends blinked in unison around the table and took consecutive breaths before diving into the interrogation.

"What's there not to like, Becky? Is it the color of the carpet? The song selections?"

"I don't know," I fumbled. "Yes. No. I don't know!"

"Is it the people? Are they not friendly?"

"Yes. No. Oh, I don't know!"

"Are you okay with your relationship with God?"

"Yes, oh, yes! It's wonderful—He's wonderful. I'm more assured of God's love than I've ever been. I'm especially enjoying a slow read through the Gospels, but I'm finding more and more that I want to read them alone, not in a Bible-study group to be analyzed with sections roped off and charted and colored. I have you all and other Christian friends I love to be with. We lunch, we pray, we share each others' lives. I come away filled and renewed. But for some reason, lately I've wanted to hibernate from church. I come away empty and relieved that the ordeal is over, my penance done. What is wrong with me?"

We talked around the subject for nearly an hour.

This morning I sit alone, sipping my coffee and staring out the window at the overcast coolness of the morning. I pull my terry cloth robe up around my neck. I mull over my unenthusiastic feelings about going to church. I find, surprisingly, there are stirrings inside similar to those of an angry little girl. The responsible parent part of my head argues back with plenty of "shoulds" and "oughts"—like the old Frosted Mini Wheats commercial where the adult on the outside battles emotions with the outspoken kid on the inside.

But this time the childish feelings prevail, and I decide to give vent to them for a change. "In middle adulthood," writes Paul Hardin in *What Are You Doing with the Rest of Your Life,* "the inner child long denied becomes increasingly insistent. It wants to be heard."

Now I've not completely bought into this "inner child" stuff—much of it smacks of a New Age excuse to be old-fashioned selfish. But I am careful not to throw out the concept of our inner child with the New Age bathwater. We are, eternally, children to our heavenly Father. Not only is this concept biblical, it is a part of us we can never outgrow. And should never want to.

Yesterday I picked up a little book where kids candidly talk about God. One young boy's insight forced the corners of my mouth into a weak smile. "When Jesus was my age, He went to church with a bunch of people and got lost. It happens." I think Jesus understands what is happening to me. I'm probably one of thousands, maybe millions, who've felt lost in church. It happens.

Still, I'm alarmed to find I am close to tears. What if I were ten years old, headstrong, honest, and outspoken? What would I be bursting to say right now? Imagine…if I were to take Jesus at His Word this morning and come to Him as a child, what would I say to Him? How would I express my feelings about church. About Him? How would it all come tumbling out? I might ramble. I might say things I shouldn't. If I were a child, sitting on the grass having a conversation with Jesus, what would I say? Perhaps I'd start with something like…

Jesus, I love You! Can we talk about this "church thing" for a minute? First of all, I don't understand why I am supposed to dress up fancy to come to church. Why do I have to wear dresses that itch, and put on shoes that hurt, and curl my hair to visit Your house? Who made up Sunday school clothes? If You meant what You said, if You want people to come to You as children, how come everybody doesn't just wear overalls and T-shirts and Keds and ponytails and baseball caps or even feety pajamas to church? And maybe even run through a mudpuddle on the way to the door? Who came up with the big idea that we should all look la-di-da for church?

I wonder about another thing. In the Bible, You got to have church outside. You visited fancy temples now and then, but maybe just to keep Your foot in the door. When it was up to You, You had church under the sky by a lake or on a grassy hill or in a boat. You didn't need fancy banners or stained-glass windows; Your sun painted the background with bursty oranges and purples and reds. You didn't need an organist playing worshipy mood music; You had the Sea of Galilee making splashy, smooth sounds with its waves dropping onto the shore. And Your birds sang from the trees in between Your words. I wish I could have gone to Your outside church.

And, Lord, there's another aspect I don't like about church: the sermons. I especially don't like the little outlines with every point starting with the same letter of the alphabet. Who teaches this stuff to preachers anyway? I don't want to hear about The Position, The Principles, and The Promise anymore. (And is there really even supposed to be just one "big teacher"?)

What I really want to know is what happened to my brothers and sisters this week. Where were they when they met with God? What words did He say to their hearts? And did they laugh, did they cry, did they sing or dance with the joy of it? I also want to hear stories. Short ones. Like the ones You told, Jesus. Children love stories. And I'll tell You something else: I think their parents do, too.

And it seems like every church should be full of nice old people—the kind whose skin has gotten too big for them so it kind of hangs wiggly under their chins. The kind who are especially nice to children. It's especially good if they keep gum or candy in their pockets to hand out after church…if moms and dads will let their kids have some. (And their moms and dads should let them have some.) I wonder, did You carry treats around in Your robe pocket just in case? It probably didn't matter if You did or not. The kids all loved You because You were kind and noticed them.

Do You know what my favorite miracle is? It was the time all those gobs of people were listening to You. They loved Your stories so much they forgot to stop and eat. Remember that time? And remember how those grown-up disciples of Yours were all stressed out because there wasn't any food? I think it is funny that You had to find Yourself a calm, quiet little kid to help You out there. Sometimes grown-ups just get in the way. I would love to have seen their faces when that boy's lunch just kept growing and growing and growing. I wonder if somebody put up golden arches later that said, "Over 5000 served from five loaves and two fishes." And You know what? I really wish I could have been with the kids on that day.

This is kind of off the subject, but I think food's a good thing to have around at church if you are going to go ahead and have a church anyway. Potluck suppers are great. Especially the coconut cake and the Mexican salad. I get very thankful for lunch when there is coconut cake and Mexican salad.

Um…back to the part I hate most about church. If You want to know the truth, church reminds me too much of school. It's too big, there are too many people, and there's too much sitting and listening. I'm not good at trying to squeeze into talking groups of people or wandering around hoping I look like I know what I'm doing.

I think certain grown-ups feel really bad admitting they don't like to go to church a whole lot because they are supposed to love being around people who love the Lord so much. But even grown-ups probably sometimes feel lost and alone in the middle of crowds. Maybe they'd like to just go get donuts and go home.

Sometimes, I wonder how people who aren't born and raised in church ever get the gumption to visit one the first time. And lots of them actually come back again. I think probably it is the real strong talkers and good dresssers that get most gungho about it, though.

Why couldn't we just skip Big Church? And then everybody who loves You could just get together at the donut shop. And they could tell each other where they met God last week, what His words sounded like to them, and whether the words made them laugh or cry or sing or dance…or yawn. Share stories, You know. Then they could pray, sing a song, and go home. If church were like this, I maybe even could do it every other day.

"Oh, grow up and get your bobby socks and patent leather shoes on," I am sure someone out there is saying. Well, I have just one thing to say to that someone: I think you are mean and ugly, and I don't like your shirt.

I think I need some milk and cookies and a long nap now.

He went back to teaching by the sea….He taught by using stories, many stories.

MARK 4:1 THE MESSAGE

13

I'm Gonna Let My Little Light Shine

Lighting Candles in the Dark

All right, all right. I've had my cookie break and nap. I'm feeling more mature, and the child in me has had her big say. I'm teasing about it, but truthfully it is a big relief to get those pent-up childlike (childish?) whines out of my system.

I believe the best way to work through problems is what I call Instant Therapy, often completed in one long lunch surrounded by friends. There are three distinct steps. First, we vent (ala the previous chapter). Next, we empathize with the "venter." (A thank you to the readers who thought, *I know just how she feels!*) And finally, we remind one another that *we are children of God,* so we hold hands in prayer and make our way to the Father, the one who always knows best.

So now, the grown-up left in charge of my mind is wondering, *What now?* The solution is not always to change churches, although that might provide temporary relief. But we all know that every single church has its own set of problems. It's only a matter of time before they surface, and we get disillusioned again.

People tend to be very candid with me, so this much I do know: I am not alone in my frustration. Church casualties, outcasts, and misfits are everywhere. And they are immensely relieved to find a sympathetic ear. In my humble opinion, we should listen to them every once in a while, that is, if the church truly wants to understand and love real people.

I had an interesting conversation with a complete stranger in a public restroom a few months ago. I had just picked up a dress from the dry cleaners, and since I had to hurry on to a speaking event, I decided to change into the dress while in the restroom of the local grocery store.

As I was digging into my makeup bag, a woman walked in, observed my dolling up, and commented, "Nice dress. You going to church?"

"No," I answered, "but I'm about to go somewhere and give a little talk, and I'll probably say some pretty good things about God. Does that count?"

She laughed a bit and said, "You know, I'd like to believe in a good God." Then quickly she confessed, "I used to go to church every Sunday. But I was so hurt by some of the people there, I've never gone back again."

I turned toward her as I finished tightening the back of an earring and gently, carefully said, "Did you ever read that story in the Bible where the mothers took their children to Jesus to be blessed? I always thought it was kind of ironic that it was the disciples, Jesus' followers, who almost kept those kids from running into Jesus' arms."

"I never thought about it that way, but it's true. And it's *His* people that make me want to avoid everything having to do with Jesus and His church."

"Just remember, Jesus is really, really different than many of His followers act. They often mean well, but lots of us still don't know what we are doing, and the church has a lot of growing to do. Please don't let Christians stop you from running to Him like a kid needing a hug. He loves you so much."

She blinked, as if to keep strong emotion at bay. Then before turning to leave she said, "Thanks, I really needed to hear that today."

I wondered, *Is it possible this woman found more compassion in our impromptu over-the-sink encounter than she'd been able to find from her years in an organized church?* The thought frustrated and angered me. It's easy to understand why so many people feel the benefits of belonging to church are not worth the pain involved. And many feel that if they left, they wouldn't be missed, kind of like taking a teaspoon of sand from the desert. *The professionals are in charge anyway. Who needs me?*

I know a wonderful, God-fearing woman who grew up in a wonderful, God-loving, church-going home. She also adored her father, who pastored one of the most well-known churches in America. Today she's married to a wonderful, God-loving, church-going man. However the "church-going" part is something she no longer feels an obligation to do. I also know a terrific counselor, a deeply spiritual, compassionate man. God's love pours through him as he comforts hurting people in his office every day. But he's also said "thank you, but no thank you" to involvement in a regular, formal church. Been there, done that, got burned, gonna avoid it again.

I have to admit there's something about their decisions I admire. In fact, we recently took a year-long sabbatical from organized church. I continued to meet with Christian friends on a regular basis; I continued to absorb and to minister in churches on weekends in my speaking travels. Our kids stayed involved in youth groups. But when I was home on Sunday morning, Scott and I spent the morning in quiet reflection—usually out of doors, reading Scripture and praying near the lake in our backyard. And then we enjoyed our Sabbath at a leisurely pace, preparing a home-cooked lunch for our kids, napping in the afternoon. It was great. And yet...after a year, we both began to miss having a place to call our "fellowship home." We knew it was time to put our big toes back into church waters again.

After all, what would happen if the traditional, organized church disappeared from the American scene? As wobbly as she is, the church holds up a torch of hope. I think of my friends Igor and Elaine, who grew up in the days of "godless, churchless" Russia. To attend an organized, underground worship service might, at any time, turn into a life-threatening event. Elaine's father, the pastor, was dragged away to prison twice for his faith. There was only one Bible in their church, and it had to be passed around in secret from family to family. When Elaine's' family got their Bible turn it was like Christmas and New Year's all rolled into one.

I realize that in so many ways I am spoiled, not remembering what a privilege it is to assemble en masse, openly, to worship our King. My husband hastens to remind me that one of the main purposes in coming together in a "big church" setting is to honor God and worship Him as a family; it is not simply about getting our human needs met.

Oh yeah, whispers the little girl in me, *I forgetted that part.*

Also, I must admit, with all its faults, the structure of a formal church gives our children healthy places to go and sweet, decent kids with whom to hang out. Because of the youth group, our teens have had opportunities to minister to orphans and the poorest of the poor on summer mission trips. I met my husband 25 years ago in a church youth group. Come to think of it, I've met most of my best, lifelong friends in some pocket of a church setting. Even the women to whom I made my I-don't-like-church confession are friends I made at—you guessed it—church.

There is no easy answer to the complexities in the body of Christ today. The bad news is that the church is imperfect. It does not meet everyone's needs; it sometimes does more harm than good. I don't even know why we refer to it as "the organized church" because it often appears anything but organized with its members fussing and fighting and pulling and pushing—often on front pages of newspapers for all the world to see and cluck their tongues at. Let's face it. Sometimes it's plain embarrassing to admit holding membership in this God-ordained family of feuders.

The good news is that since the church is already imperfect, it won't shake things up much if the likes of you and me join in. Often, too, there are moments of glory when the church responds from its heart and does a great deal of good. Mother Teresa and her tender work among lepers was sanctioned and funded by a church. (Maybe not your particular denomination, but still, part of the church universal.) During the Nazi reign, Corrie ten Boom and members of her church risked and gave their lives to save Jewish families and friends.

Ironically, my hometown of Greenville, Texas, was recently blasted across national headlines and "honored" with visits from the New Black Panthers and the Ku Klux

Klan. (I've yet to hear of one citizen, black or white, who welcomes either group here.) I stood in our high-school football stadium Sunday night, looking out over a salt-and-pepper sea of thousands of black and white Christians praying together as Dr. Tony Evans led us in a call to unity and peace. There were few dry eyes as the crowd joined hands singing "Bind us together, Lord." It is in these shining moments that I know that this mystery called "the body of Christ" has all the potential to be the eyes, hands, and compassion of Jesus to a confused and angry world. If only church happened like this every Sunday. If only it did not take an enemy's assault to bind us together with love.

Last night I felt something stuck down the side of my mattress and, curious as to the origin of the lump, I fished around and pulled it out. It was my well-worn paperback copy of *Disappointment with God* by Philip Yancey. (Whole libraries of used books and drawers full of socks and bags full of cookie crumbs live between the mattresses and under my bed. We could sustain our family for months, I believe, from the haphazard rations pushed, swept, shoved, and stored there.)

I'm a huge Yancey fan in the same way some people are Dallas Cowboys fans. I am eternally grateful to this thoughtful, honest, intelligent, fuzzy-haired brother in Christ. He has a way of putting so much that is puzzling about the Christian life, about God, about pain, about the Bible into meaningful chunks I can slowly, methodically digest. *The Jesus I Never Knew* is perhaps the most significant book I have ever read. And I can't wait to read his *Soul Survivor,* about how his own faith survived the rough waters of church attendance. Philip and I have had some tidbits of empathetic correspondence about this issue over the past few years.

I found myself scanning the pages of *Disappointment* and, as always, I gleaned fresh insight from Yancey's pen. "Dorothy Sayers has said that God underwent three great humiliations in His efforts to rescue the human race," he writes. "The first was the Incarnation, when He took on the confines of a physical body. The second was the Cross, when He suffered the ignominy of public execution. The third humiliation," Sayers suggested, "is the Church. In an awesome act of self-denial, God entrusted His reputation to ordinary people."

Oh. So, let me get this straight, Philip.

God Almighty is trusting ordinary, quirky people like me? A woman/child whiner like me? To represent the love and compassion of the Divine Christ? *Wow.* The little girl in me raises her tiny, wavering voice in protest: "I think maybe God should know I'm not big enough for this important of a job. Maybe He should think it over a little longer."

It dawns on me, astonishes me, as I slowly realize we humans not only place our faith in God, but He has also chosen to place His faith in us.

I wonder what would happen if we, the church, would just remember that we aren't really so great or important— nor do we *have* to be. We're just a plain, ordinary bunch of kids whose job is to let our little lights shine by pointing the way to the warmth and love of our Omnipotent Father, the one who always knows best.

Be imitators of God, therefore, as dearly loved children and live a life of love....Live as children of light.

EPHESIANS 5:1-2, 8

14

Can We Play in the Mud?

The Joy of Getting Your Hands Dirty

Mud...glorious mud.

Remember the feel of squish-squashy stuff oozing up between your toes? Who knows how many chefs began their careers by decorating fancy mud pies with chocolate dirt and candy rocks and twig candles. (My family says my baked goodies still have something of an earthy-rocky-twiggy tang.)

I'd almost forgotten what wonderful amusement a bit of dirt and water can provide for a child. And how large pools of gushy, goopy, glorious mud can entertain children of all ages for hours at a time. That is, until last week, when a little boy down the street reminded me what excitement awaits those who take the time go outside and play in the mud. I should probably mention that "the little boy down the street" is Wally, a six-foot grandfather of seven.

Let me quickly set the stage before I give you the scoop on this story. Our family lives on the bank of a small lake in a neighborhood of about 100 cabins that dot the surrounding woods. Living on water has been an adventure in and of itself, but one of the most interesting events in our neighborhood happens when the board members of our community decide it is time to drain the lake for dock repairs, or to plant fish-attracting algae, or, I suspect, simply to satisfy curiosities about what's lurking under the water. One thing is certain: The best thing lurking is mud. The thickest, goopiest doggone best mud a young boy or old man could ever hope to squish-squash around in.

Temporarily, there is no boating, skiing, fishing, or swimming, but our children are far from depressed when the water is drained. They now have invented a new sport of their own to play during these times of forced lake drought. It's called "muddin'." "What's muddin'?" you ask. Perhaps I should simply explain how muddin' is carried out, and I think you'll get the general idea.

To get the best out of the muddin' experience, you first pull on the tallest pair of rubber boots you can find—hip boots are best. Then, starting from the shore, the object of the game is to wade toward the middle of what used to be the lake, venturing out and in as deep as you dare. Our teenagers routinely make it clear up to their necks in black goop. And that's about the gist of it.

Why would anyone in his or her right mind want to do this? I don't know. Believe me, I don't know! I was a child of more dainty constitution, but my kids absolutely love this activity. Since muddin' keeps them happy and busy and out of my hair, and since I suppose it's an invigorating form of isometric exercise, I hold my tongue. As long as they spray off with the hose in the yard before setting a toe on my carpet, I'm pretty easy-going about such things. I inherited this attitude, I think, from my own mother. She never blinked about letting us kids play outside in the rain. In reference to such leniencies (or lunacies, as the case may be), one of my boys once complimented me by saying, "Mom, I'm so glad you aren't sensible like other mothers." "Thank Granny," I replied.

There is one thing I protest about the muddin' days, however. Every now and then one of my children will dig up and bring into the house a horrible, vile-looking, hissing eel-like creature, about a foot long and an inch-and-a-half thick. They find them burrowing into the mud along the banks. The critters go by the name of "mud puppies" around here, much too sweet a name for these miniature horror monsters if you ask me. They give me the heebie-jeebies and look just like offspring of those blood-sucking earth eels from the movie *Tremors.*

Once Gabriel brought a small mud puppy into the bathroom and left it unattended in some tap water in the sink. I didn't realize it was there, so I just reached into the sink to pull the plug. Before that fat eel disappeared down the drain like slick fettuccini, he managed to slither around my hand just to let me know he was there. As you might expect, I screamed until there were no screams left in me. Now I have a permanent case of the jitters. I keep expecting that someday a slimy black creature will return and pop its hissing head up out of the sink—just when I least expect it. And I will simply die, that's all. I'll just die.

Now, back to Wally. It seems Wally thought it would be a great idea, while the water was down, to dig some deep pools around the edge of the lake—pools where fish could eventually congregate so fishermen could eventually do the same. In truth, I strongly suspect Wally simply had a hankering to dig a big hole with a great big tractor. And so, when his wife went shopping and promised to be gone for the entire morning, Wally set out to go play in the mud with his man-sized Tonka truck.

In our neighborhood, the sound of a tractor or backhoe's engine on a Saturday morning is like the call of a roaring pied piper to every machine-loving male within hearing distance. So it wasn't long before Wally had a crowd of playmates around him, eager to help or at least to provide him with an audience. It goes without saying that as soon as the sound of a heavy-duty engine drifted through the backdoor, Scott walked outside toward the noise like some beguiled sleepwalker in a cartoon—not blinking, not uttering a word. On his hypnotic trek toward the Big Machine Noise, Scott ran into Jim Ed, our no-nonsense, laid-back neighbor.

"Hey, Jim Ed!" Scott called. "What's goin' on down there by the lake?"

"Wally thinks he's going to dig himself a fishin' hole," Jim Ed replied. "I tried to tell him it was still too muddy."

"So what are you going to do now?" Scott asked.

"Well," drawled Jim Ed, "guess I'll pour me a cup of coffee and come sit out here on the porch. Then I think I'll watch a tractor sink."

You know, we all found out that Jim Ed's not only no-nonsense and laid-back—he's smart. He sat down just in time to see Wally drive the tractor six feet out from the edge of the mud and watch it sink nearly six feet under. Talk about your mud on your face. Wally was in it at least up to his hip boots, and Scott walked back in the house to give an updated blow-by-blow report.

"Becky," he informed me, "Wally's going to have to rent a big diesel truck to come pull that tractor out. Can you believe it?" I could tell my husband was working hard at trying to disguise the little-boy excitement that kept threatening to creep into his manly, serious voice.

"Honey," I answered brightly, "I think it is just wonderful of Wally to do this on a holiday so all you neighborhood guys can be in on this while you've got time off to enjoy it. You couldn't pay for better male bonding experiences than this—men, mud, big tractors, and trucks. Shall I make popcorn?"

"No time," Scott answered, no longer attempting to hide his grin, "I gotta get back out there! Tell the boys to get up out of bed; they'll want to see this!"

That evening, I visited with Wally's wife. She was sitting on the couch, staring numbly off into space, shaking her head back and forth, and mumbling.

"Five hours," she said over and over again to herself. "I only left him alone for five hours..."

Bless her heart. We women are going to have to pull together, I can tell. Until that mud is covered up once again with lake, I'm afraid none of us can completely relax. All we can do is try to keep a better eye on our kids—large and small—while they play in the goopy, squishy, gushy, glorious, eternally magnetic mud.

● ● ●

After reading this story, and admitting to finding it a mite funny, Wally wrote me the following note.

> I do want to set the record straight, however. *We did get one fishing hole!!* When that big diesel truck

upsurged the tractor, it left *a pretty nice bass hole.* Not a big one and we don't want to estimate dollars per cubic feet, but it will provide a home for several lake bass.

Consider the record straightened!

God, save me, because the water has risen to my neck. I'm sinking down into the mud, and there is nothing to stand on. I am in deep water.

PSALM 69:1-2 NCV

What Does God Do? God makes bees with little wings all day. Probably out of mud.

Dandi Daley MacKall,
Children Say the Greatest Things About God

15

Fixin' Stuff

Boys Will Be Handymen

fter a long day of playing handyman around the house, Scott plopped his tired body down in the old green rocker in my office. Ever since he was a little boy, Scott has been "fixin' stuff." And only the Lord can help the woman who even so much as suggests he might hire a professional. Fixin' stuff is my man's sacred territory, his boyish realm of "I can do it myself."

For a few seconds Scott just sat and rocked, grateful for a respite as I finished up some editing. I typed in the last correction, swiveled my chair around, and propped my feet up on my husband's weary knees.

"Tired?" I asked.

"Exhausted," he answered, staring blankly ahead.

"So now that you are here, I suppose you'd better go ahead and tell me the news. Do we have water? And if we do, is it hot, cold, or lukewarm? And I'm almost afraid to ask but…" I gazed upward at this point, my hands folded together. "Lord, have mercy on us, do we have a clothes dryer yet?" I crossed my fingers and shut my eyes tightly as I waited in suspense for the reply.

I should explain that for three weeks now, we've been without a clothes dryer. Actually we've always been without a legitimate clothes dryer. I bought the machine used—well used—from a local Laundromat for the bargain price of $20. For our 20 big ones we got a harvest-gold machine that looked and sounded more like a giant rock tumbler than a clothes dryer. But these are the things you put up with when you are raising four kids on a tight budget.

In the beginning, the dryer sounded as if it were tossing about a few small pebbles. Then it went through a period of time when the pebble-tumbling noises actually came to a halt, which would have been a relief except that our mechanically deranged appliance had other tricks up its belt. At that point our clothes tumbler went from merely drying our clothes to baking them. Honestly. White dress shirts began popping out of the steel door the color of perfectly browned toast. During this awkward stage of dryerhood, our clothes always smelled like they'd been dried at the end of a coat hanger over a campfire.

Finally Scott figured out how to adjust the temperature from bake/broil to normal, but then the rock-tumbling noises returned. Only this time the sound had graduated from mere namby-pamby pebble bumping to serious boulder grinding. We knew the dryer's days were numbered when Jim Ed, our next-door neighbor, came over and asked Scott if we could hear the horrible noise our "air conditioner" was making outside. Scott had to confess that the ruckus Jim Ed had been hearing was not emitting from an outside AC unit, but from inside our laundry room's clothes dryer. I was sure it would blow at any moment, but for several more weeks it noisily, but efficiently, managed to keep our clothes dry. Finally, however, the hunk of metal clanked to a grinding halt. But, hey, we figured we'd certainly milked our 20 bucks out of it.

You may not believe this, but we actually had already purchased a nice, almost-new dryer. It was sitting on the back porch waiting for the old machine to give up the ghost so it could move in on its territory. "Why in the world," you might be wondering, "did we wait so long to replace Old Yeller?"

I'll tell you why. Because the new, improved dryer runs on propane. And before we could install it, for reasons only a husband can understand, we would have to let our butane tank temporarily run out of fuel. Why? So he could move the tank over to the side of the house. *Oh.* And if he were going to move the butane tank over to the side of the house, he would also need to go ahead and move the water tank from the bathroom to the laundry room. I hope this is making sense to you. And if he had to do that, well then, all sorts of plumbing lines and gizmos and connectors and such would have to be moved and welded and soldered and piped. "This could take days," Scott had been ominously predicting. Faced with this scenario, I agreed with my husband that the most logical thing to do under the circumstances was to stall as long as humanly possible.

This weekend however, with the expiring of the old dryer, the jig was up.

For the last four days, in addition to air-drying our laundry on the back porch like a family of hillbillies, we've also been coping without benefit of hot water—in January.

Over this weekend I've not seen either of Scott's hands without tools attached to them, and I've only caught brief glimpses of his face from behind bars and under pipes. He's grown the scraggly beginnings of a beard. His eyes have taken on a hollow, haunted look, and all his attempts at conversation have started with, "Becky, please tell me you've seen a little piece of metal that looks like an elbow" or "a donut" or "your grandfather's nose."

"Becky," he confessed in a tone that sounded near surrender, "I think I've had my fill of fixing stuff now."

"Do you want me to hire a—"

"Don't say it! Don't even *think* it. Give me time. I'll get my second wind."

And me? Oh, I've been pressing bravely on. I've devised an ingenious system, I think, for still managing to get my daily hot bath. I can go without almost anything, but anyone who knows me well knows I will not be deprived of my daily hot soak in the tub if I can help it. My system?

First I begin by putting four of my biggest pots on the stovetop to boil (we have an electric stove, thank goodness), and I heat one big bowl of water in the microwave.

Then I take off all my clothes (so as not to waste precious seconds when the stage is set), wrap a towel around me, and shuffle back and forth from the kitchen to the bathroom until I've emptied three gallons of boiling water into the bathtub. (Of course this has attracted a bit of attention from my children's visiting friends. "Hey, what's your mom cookin' in the bathroom? Does she always wear a towel when she boils water?")

Then I refill the pots, set them all back on the stove to boil again, and jump in the tub before the water cools off. Midway through my bath, when my hair is all lathered up with shampoo, I pop out of the tub to repeat the running back and forth with hot pads and pots of boiling water in order to reheat the two inches of bathwater that have begun to cool.

See? Nothin' to it.

So now you understand how much I had vested in the answers I was about to receive from my bone-weary, handy husband. The news was mixed.

"Becky," he began solemnly, like Colin Powell at a military briefing, "as it now lines up, yes, we have a working clothes dryer."

"Hallelujah!"

"Yes, there is hot and cold running water in the bathtub."

"Oh, Baby, I knew you could do it!"

"However, there is no water at all in any of the bathroom sinks."

"Yuuuuck…"

"In the kitchen, I have hot water only coming out of the faucet."

"That I can live with."

"No water to the dishwasher."

"That I cannot. What about the washing machine?"

"Cold only."

"All in all, Sir," I replied with a dutiful salute, "not too shabby. The troops will survive. For a couple of days. But I cannot write another word tonight. May I be dismissed to my appointment with a tub of steaming hot water?"

● ● ●

The Following Day

It was rather amusing this morning to watch the ¹ fighting over who got to use the bathtub first—to brush teeth and wet their combs. I went to the kitchen si⌐

cold drink of water and forgot that today's option from that particular source was limited to hot liquids only. Resigned, I put a tea bag in a cup of steaming water from the hydrant. As it was steeping, I glanced out the kitchen window when, what to my wondering eyes should appear—but a white commode on the lawn. Surely not...

I walked straight out the door in my morning robe and sure enough, there in front of God and the neighbors and everybody sat a porcelain potty.

I did a quick about face and marched back in the house.

"Look, Scott," I stated in no uncertain terms, "I'm a very patient woman. I'm okay with table saws and towers of pink insulation stacked on my front porch. I can even handle a dryer on the back porch. But I draw the line at a lawn potty!"

"Gee, Beck," Scott answered calmly, sounding strangely like the character Tim on *Home Improvement*. "I just needed to spray it off. No need to get upset."

"Yeah, well, it's my potty and I'll cry if I want to!"

One look at my face and Scott knew I meant business. I'd reached my fix-it-man limit. As the kids and I loaded up the station wagon for the drive to their school, I saw Scott run out the front door (in nothing but his boxer shorts), pick up the commode, and drag it to the front porch. Then he threw a blanket over it for camouflage.

I looked helplessly at the kids.

Zeke couldn't resist. He rolled down the window and shouted, "Hey, Dad, try putting a hat on it!"

Rachel followed up with, "And a carrot nose and a corncob pipe might look nice!"

Scott snickered and darted back into the house. I just shook my head.

He is taking off a few days to work on the house and get it in shape for a Friday-night pizza party for the kids' youth group. Hopefully, all our faucets will be running hot and cold again by then. (If not, it is safe to assume my blood will be.)

● ● ●

In rereading this chapter I laughed out loud as I remembered those building-our-home days, recognizing afresh that the most exasperating experiences often make the funniest family stories in the retelling.

I'm pleased to report that after ten years of scrimping and sawing, our two-story Victorian-style home (aka: The House that Scott Built) is *almost* complete. (Alas, I'm still negotiating for a set of stairs in place of the rope and rock-climbing wall.)

And...my propane propelled dryer still works! (So well, in fact, that last week my handy husband deposited $300 worth of my dry-clean-only clothes in it and they came out beautifully. Now, if I can just find some toddler who needs a few nice linen business suits....)

Tonight, however, I went to take a bath and quickly discovered (after my hair and torso were doused from above) that the knobbie-thingie that shifts the water from the shower head to the bathtub spigot is not doing its knobbie-thingie job.

Scott was reading a book when I informed him of this new problem, and he practically leapt for his toolbox—a handyman on a mission! A boy with a screwdriver ready to fix somethin'.

I have to take a moment in all this teasing to brag on my handy guy, whose "real job" is to oversee creative building projects for the national, nonprofit organization Girl Scouts USA. (We like to say he does Guy Stuff for the Girl Scouts.)

At Camp Bette Perot (named for Ross Perot's feisty, benevolent sister), Scott recently designed and oversaw the building of an incredible, half-million-dollar tree house project.

As his wife, I've seen the wonderful things my husband can create, but I was open-mouthed when I saw what he had orchestrated this time. We walked through what looks like the enormous trunk of a tree into a gorgeous Swiss Family Robinson style complex with a central meeting hall and catwalks to individual bunkhouses. The architecture is such that everything, from the rafters to the windows, gives you the feeling you are inside a giant oak.

We recently heard the Tree House Project was to be featured in *Texas Architectural Digest,* and Scott's going to receive an award this month from the Texas forestry department on "best creative use of natural materials in a building."

I don't think I've ever seen my husband look happier, younger, and healthier than the spring he had this design in his mind, a toolbox in his truck, and the opportunity to work with other fun and talented guys building a tree house. (Wouldn't this be any boy's fantasy job?)

Now I am blessed to see my husband's craftsmanship legacy passed on. This month Scott is helping our son Zeke and his wife, Amy, build their first home. It's unique and creative since Zeke designed it using cedar and rock with a green tin roof. I see the same light in Zeke's eyes that his father has when he's "on a project." (Zeke is also working on a degree in architecture, much to Scott's delight.)

So here they are, father and son, whistling while they work. As long as they have a hammer in one hand and a nail in the other, they're happy.

"Where did this man get this wisdom and these miraculous powers?" they asked. "Isn't this the carpenter's son?"

MATTHEW 13:54-55

16

Will You Go with Me?

Freely Asking for Help

A magazine cover caught my eye the other day. On the front was a photograph of a little boy and girl, both dressed in grown-up attire: business suits, briefcases, the whole bit. The question across the top of the picture asked, "Are you grown-up yet?" Then, in parentheses, it also asked, "Do you know anyone who is?"

Am I grown-up? Well, that all depends on your definition. If grown-up means you can have your own quarters and eat dessert first, hey, I'm as adult as they come. But if, by any chance, being grown-up means you are a responsible, competent, out-of-town traveler, you might as well bring me my blankie and cookies and milk right now. Frankly, I still need a lot of help getting out of town and back again. Not only do I depend on the kindness of strangers, I cling closely to my more travel-savvy friends.

One of the biggest challenges and changes in my life is that now that I am a real live author I'm getting invitations to travel and give real live speeches. The first obstacle I had to overcome was my fear of *flying*. Of course, it isn't really that I was afraid of flying; it was the *falling* part that got to me. But I'm much, much better now. Only rarely does the flight attendant have to dig my fingernails out of the person's arm sitting next to me.

The second hurdle hasn't been as easy for me to jump. Because of what Gabe so succinctly pointed out at the start of this book—the part about my having no sense—out-of-state travel poses a special challenge. There are a few basic skills that would, I'm sure, increase my confidence level as I try finding my way around a strange city—for instance, the ability to read a map.

I've been blessed thus far to have friends who are so desperate to get away they've been willing to take me on as a traveling companion to sort of show me the touristy ropes. Little did they know what they were committing themselves to. My problem with traveling is this: Once I hit the airport, I transform responsibility-wise to a five-year-old child. Thus, the person traveling with me begins a subtle, but predictable, evolvement into the parent.

Tina Jacobsen was one of my first traveling buddies. Tina owns a burgeoning publicity business (that at this time was burgeoning right out of her home) called Books and Bookings. The first time we ever talked on the phone, Tina's young daughter walked into her office during our conversation. I guess she was tossing her shoe or something because it flew straight up in the air, and when it came down it hit her square on the head.

"Becky," said Tina over her daughter's crying in the background, "I just read your book, and I'm so glad I'm talking to you right now. I know I don't have to put on my executive voice and panic if my kids make a racket in the background."

From that point, we hit it off and have become good friends—making a regular lunch date in Dallas to discuss publishing and marketing, "wifeing" and mothering, and trying to operate a professional business with family wandering in and out of our offices. So when we both had business to conduct in Nashville, Tina agreed to go with me to help me learn the ropes of business travel.

I met her at the Dallas/Fort Worth airport. When it was our turn to board the plane, Tina asked, "Becky, now where is your ticket?" Already, her voice had picked up a faint maternal quality.

"It's in my purse, don't worry," I replied with a grin.

"O.K.," said Tina. "Don't get offended by this but I have read your books. Where is your purse?"

"Well, it is right—*oh no!* I don't know! Oh, my goodness, it has more than $300 in cash and my airplane ticket in it!"

Tina swallowed hard, checked her watch, and then asked me very carefully where I had been in the last few minutes.

"The restroom! I went to the ladies room!"

Running full speed ahead I darted to the ladies room and there, miraculously, sitting in the sink was my open purse. Right where I'd left it. Not one penny was missing. I praised God from the top of my lungs and caught up with Tina just in time to board the plane.

I learned my lesson right away and held on to my purse from then on as if my life depended on it. I did very well, too, until we got to the restaurant in Nashville. We had a lovely time, and as we turned to leave, I double-checked to make sure I had my purse swinging over my shoulder. Then Tina asked calmly, "Becky, are you missing anything?"

"Nope," I answered, with childlike confidence. "See, I've got my purse right here. My head is attached to my body. Everything is *under control*."

"Why don't you check under the table, just in case."

And there, where I had been sitting, lay five, crisp, $20 bills.

"Ooops," I apologized, sheepishly retrieving the cash off the floor. "Guess I need to start remembering to zip up my purse, huh?"

"Becky," Tina asked as we started to leave, "you *are* older than me, right?"

"By a couple of years, I think."

"Then why do I suddenly feel like your mother?"

"Don't worry. This always happens when I go on trips with people. I should have warned you."

"Right. Well, then, do you need to go potty before we leave?"

● ● ●

My next willing travel victim was my neighbor from the boonies, Melissa. Our first out-of-town trip started off smoothly enough. We boarded the plane without a hitch, laughing and talking the entire first leg of the journey. However, the challenge began when we had to pick up our luggage before changing planes in Phoenix.

We retrieved our bags with no problems, but then we had to descend on an escalator, and both of us were loaded to our necks with luggage. I don't know what possessed Melissa to do this, but she insisted I go first.

When I reached the bottom of the escalator, I managed to step off fairly gracefully. Unfortunately, my suitcase was heavier than I realized, and I couldn't drag it off with me. There it sat, like a roadblock, stuck on the bottom step. Which meant that Melissa had to descend the escalator with bags under each arm and *straddle* my suitcase to keep from falling on her face. She was also, I might add, wearing a dress. The whole scene struck me as extremely amusing. Unfortunately when I get really, really tickled I become completely incapacitated. I was literally sitting on the airport floor laughing so hard that tears were falling down both cheeks. Melissa, on the other hand, did not seem to find the situation quite as amusing. That's when her voice began to take on the maternal tone.

"Get up off that floor and come help me right now, Becky!" (I really expected her to add, "Young Lady!")

Eventually, I pulled myself up and managed to offer some weak assistance. Thankfully it didn't take long for Melissa to get tickled too, and she forgave me.

On our return trip, I boarded the plane with several pieces of take-on luggage and one shopping bag full of huge cinnamon rolls, each of them the size of a cantaloupe. We'd promised our children a treat, and these monster rolls seemed perfect. As we were squeezing down the aisle and trying to locate our seats, the bottom of my shopping bag broke loose.

"Uh-oh," I said quietly. Melissa's eyes widened with disbelief. Like a dozen bowling balls gone wild, the cinnamon rolls were veering crazily down the alley and under the seats, with passengers yelling, "Catch that one coming toward you!" and "There goes one under your feet!"

Melissa looked at the flight attendant, rolled her eyes upward, and as she watched me scrambling for the cinnamon balls said, "Kids! Whadaya gonna do with 'em?"

● ● ●

A year later, Melissa's memories of traveling with me had faded somewhat, and besides, she was desperate to break loose from the sticks for a while. This time, we were heading to sunny California. Like Lucy and Ethel, we were humming bars of "California, Here We Come" as we debarked our plane at John Wayne Airport.

After my speaking engagement was finished, we checked ourselves into a budget hotel and spent the next few days doing the tourist thing: Universal Studios (where we lingered for an hour at the "Tribute to Lucy" display), Mann's Chinese Theater (where I had my picture taken with John Wayne's boot prints), and Beverly Hills (where we ate lunch and gawked). Amazingly, I managed to behave like a responsible young lady the entire trip, and Melissa had even begun to relax. Almost.

Our budget hotel was the epitome of economy (the swimming pool was the size of my kitchen table), but it did have a whirlpool bathtub. And after a long day of touristing, I was anxious to give that whirlpool a whirl. So I flipped a switch on the wall, positioned myself in the tub, laid back and let the steaming water pour in. I couldn't wait to feel those scrubbing bubbles work their magic on my aching muscles.

Then something unusual happened. Something for which I was totally unprepared. Water began shooting out of the little holes on the side of the tub like a fountain. As a matter of fact, the jets began propelling eight-foot streams upward and all around me, hitting the wall, the ceiling, and soaking the towels. And then that horrible thing happened again—I got tickled. I could not move; I could not speak. I could hear Melissa pounding on the door, but I could not answer her. All I could do was cuddle up in a ball and snicker and snort.

"Becky! Answer me!" Melissa was yelling outside the bath-room door. "Are you O.K.? I hear something slapping against the wall! There is *water* pouring out from under the *door!*"

Still I could not catch my breath as I sat like one of those cherub statues encased in a huge fountain of water. The noise of the whirlpool drowned out my feeble attempts to communicate. Finally, Melissa opened the door a couple of inches. Streams of water hit her—splat—in the face. As a matter of fact, the water shot out so hard and so high that it arched over her head, soaking one of the headboards and bedspreads out in the hotel room.

"I won't look," promised Melissa as her arm stretched toward the whirlpool button, "but I'm reaching in and turning this thing off!"

Immediately, the indoor hurricane died down, and we surveyed the damage. An inch of water puddled on the floor and beads of water dripped from every conceivable surface. The towels were completely saturated. Melissa smoothed a lock of damp hair on her forehead. The maternal voice returned.

"Becky, did you read the instructions?"

"What instructions?"

"The ones on the bathtub that say, first fill the tub up with water until it covers the jets, *then* turn the whirlpool button on."

"Oh, those instructions."

Melissa made me vow not to touch any more buttons without her permission. And added that tomorrow, if I were very, very good, she'd take me with her to Disneyland.

Entreat me not to leave you, or to turn back from following after you, for wherever you go, I will go; and wherever you lodge, I will lodge.

RUTH 1:16 NKJV

17

Let's Go to the Magic Kingdom!

Innocent Wisdom

A t the end of a speaking engagement in California, a woman came up and asked me if I'd like a couple of free tickets to Disneyland.

"Well," I explained, "I'm just here with a friend of mine. We don't have our kids with us."

"Oh," she said with a grin and a wink, as she handed me the tickets, "you'll *really* have fun, then!"

And so that's how Melissa and I ended up walking through the gates of Disney's Magic Kingdom as exhausted adults. We came back out that same entrance, several hours later, as exuberant children.

My friend Melissa and I flew above rooftops in Never-Neverland. We sat entranced at the intricate detail and diversity of the famous "It's a Small World" ride. (Though I believe if I had to hear the chorus of that repetitive song one more time I might go out of my small, small mind.) I wondered, perplexed, at the new virtual reality rides. *How do they do that? How do they make you feel as though you've just sped through galaxies in a starship?*

But my favorite part of all was the parade. Not just any parade, the "Lion King" parade. Disney style. Never in all my life have I seen such a gorgeous display, such beautiful music, right where I could reach out and touch it. In spite of the grown-up within, I found myself caught up in the fantastic display as dancers of all nationalities in brilliant costumes ascended poles and floats and swayed to the beautiful rhythms of the song, "The Circle of Life."

By evening, the transformation was complete: I was a grinning fool sporting a Mickey Mouse shirt and a matching beanie complete with propeller.

"Melissa," I said to my friend as we stopped for a rest and a bite to eat, "look at me! Can you believe I've bought into the whole commercialized deal—Cap'n Hook, line, and sinker?"

"I noticed," said Melissa, aiming a camera in my mouse-eared direction. "It happens to the best of us. Face it, Becky. You've been Disneyed."

We found a table near a jazz band and dance floor and propped our weary feet on a nearby chair. The band started up, playing the romantic, toe-tapping music of the 1940s. Melissa and I visited with some teenagers during the break, who were elegantly dressed in 40s regalia. They'd been having a ball, swing stepping together under the stars. (They told us they come out several times a week just for some good, wholesome fun. I know, they could have knocked us over with a feather, too.)

The breeze was soft around my face. The gentle wind-caress gave me a twinge of homesickness. I wished...okay, yes, "upon a star"—that my husband could have been there with me at that moment. He'd have had me out on that dance floor in no time. And we'd have given those young whippersnappers a run for their money.

From the corner of my eye, I could see a young father buying his little boy some ice cream. The child reached up for the cone, his chubby hand eager for the cold, dripping sweetness. Then the band, in the background, began playing one of my favorite songs. Slow and sweet, its melody melted the simple smile of the evening into my memory. For I believe Louis Armstrong captured for all time the essence of childlike joy when he flashed his famous grin and gifted us with his rendition of "It's a Wonderful World."

As the last strains of music wound down, the little boy finished off his last bite of ice cream. Just as the raspy-voiced crooner sang the final "What – a won – der – ful world," the child, as if on cue, clapped his sticky hands together. Grinning for all he was worth, he looked straight at me and shouted, *"Yeah!"*

And I looked at him and shouted, *"Yeah!"* right back at him.

And for that enchanted moment, connecting on some kind of kid frequency, the world indeed seemed sparkling and amazing and completely wonderful. Louis would have been pleased.

● ● ●

I've been pondering a metaphor since my day at Disney-land: It is the grown-ups who buy the tickets and guide their children to enter into the "Magic Kingdom."

But in the "Kingdom of God," according to Jesus, the roles are reversed. It is the children who hold the tickets and point the way for us grown-ups to humbly, delightedly, and wholeheartedly enter into all the kingdom's riches.

It's a paradox of life I've discovered as a parent. I thought I was placed here to guide and teach my children, but more and more often I wonder if God has placed children in our midst to teach *us*.

But Jesus called the children to him and said, "Let the little children come to me, and do not hinder them, for the kingdom of God belongs to such as these. I tell you the truth, anyone who will not receive the kingdom of God like a little child will never enter it."

Luke 18:16-17

I myself have been flattered by the reputation for never having quite grown up.
Walt Disney

18

Watch Me Sing and Dance!

Intrigue with Music and Movement

I met a kid at a recent local folk festival. He was having an absolute ball playing around with a couple of sticks—in front of anybody who'd pause long enough to watch the show. So I asked this kid, "How old are you anyway?"

"I turned 70 this year," he answered with a grin.

This gentleman was one of several lively senior citizens Scott and I met that day. They didn't appear to be ready for retirement homes, although several seemed likely candidates for kindergarten—especially a kindergarten that allowed for plenty of playtime. It was the first time in 20 years I found myself thinking, *I can't wait till I get older!*

The stick kid's real name turned out to be Donald de Camp, but he goes by "Mr. Bones." This was evident because the word "Bones" was engraved on the back of his leather belt. (Leather belts substitute for business cards and billboards among folk-festival types.) He goes by "Mr. Bones" because he plays the bones. Not the ones attached to his skeleton, but two pieces of birds-eye maple carved into the shape and size of a couple of thick bookmarks.

Held loosely between the fingers they snap out infinite and complicated rhythms to the harmonies of guitars, banjos, dulcimers, and such. Mr. Bones played his sticks two sets at a time—a pair going in each hand. I must say it was an awe-inspiring sight for all who watched this performer at work.

Scott and I took advantage of an opportunity to visit with Bones during a break. As the old gentleman wiped the sweat from his forehead he said, "Man, oh man, I *love* that rhythm!" Now he wasn't referring to a particular rhythm in a particular song. He loved the big idea of rhythm, the entire concept of rhythm—any regular beat that allowed him the chance to get out his sticks and play.

He told us that years ago the "bones" were originally made from animal bones, and he'd even found some evidence that "the bones," as musical instruments, had been in existence some 1500 years before Christ. Young Donald picked them up as a child for the pure fun of it and has been playing them ever since.

That's all the information we could squeeze out of our conversation because the band started back up again, and all his friends began begging him to come out and play with them some more. He bowed his apologies to us young'ins, shuffled to center stage, closed his eyes for a moment, then went to tapping and dancing and playing those bones. He was wild joy on the loose.

Scott's eyes followed Bones' every movement. (My husband has always been an admirer of old codgers, especially the ones with plenty of twinkles left in their eyes.)

I imagine if Scott were to write a male version of the famous poem, "When I Am Old I Shall Wear Purple," it might go something like this:

When I am old, I shall wear my hair in tufts of sweepy silver 'round the perimeter of my head.

I shall wear old boots and faded jeans and a tanned leather belt with my name on the back.

I shall own a crisp white shirt, a black string tie, a handsome vest, and a pocket watch with a gold chain that loops in front.

I shall close my eyes when I hear the band start up, and I shall wander toward the sounds until the beat collides with the joy in my heart.

And I shall dance.

Alone or with a pretty gal or with my best set of bones.

And I shall make all the young ones wish they were old—

Old enough to shuffle center stage and play

With the abandon of an uninhibited soul.

Sometime after our encounter with Bones, we heard the sound of a soulful tenor drifting above the crowd. It was accompanied by an instrument that sounded something like the warble of a bird or a woman's voice. Following the beautiful strains, we came upon a most unlikely sight. A rather dapper gentleman (even though he was clad in overalls), was sitting and playing a handsaw. He held the handsaw tucked under one thigh and ran a violin's bow across the smooth side of the blade, producing an almost otherworldly melody.

This unusual musician was also the source of the incredible tenor voice. Many of us in the crowd stood misty-eyed, listening to that voice tenderly pouring the words to "Danny Boy" from his soul into ours. Only a true Irishman could evoke the sort of emotion this man pulled from the small audience around him. He finished up the last strains a capella, ending the final notes with a gallant sweeping of the black derby from his head and over his heart.

We gave the Irishman our compliments during a break and discovered he went by the name of Ramblin' Ray Rickets. He hailed from Arkansas, and his Southern accent was void of any hint of an Irish brogue. But, sure and sure, he was Irish of soul. He said he could sing "Danny Boy" every day of his life and never grow tired of it.

As we'd done with Mr. Bones, we asked Ray how he came to play his unusual instrument. He smiled and smoothed back his hair with his hand before replacing the derby atop its silvery perch.

"It was really simple. I heard our preacher play the saw one Sunday in our li'l ol' country church, and I went up right after the service and asked him if he'd show me how to do it. Right then and there the preacher sat down and gave me a quick lesson—and I was hooked. Took it right up and never put it down."

I could see Scott making a mental list of notes, a list I knew he'd eventually bring to a hardware store: birds-eye maple, new handsaw, violin bow. Later in the afternoon, we passed table after table of wood carvings and visited with elderly craftsmen as they carved their works from butternut, maple, and other delicious-sounding woods. These men, too, were a friendly, most contented-looking lot. Scott added "a porch swing, butternut, and whittlin' knife" to his growing list of necessities. (He plans to get a running start on ol' codgerdom.)

Watching all the fiddlin', and whittlin', and cloggin', and sawin' made us suddenly aware we were hungry. Two dishes of homemade vanilla ice cream hit the spot and satisfied our hunger. Well, almost. Of course, there was no way I could pass the funnel cake booth with its swirls of fried bread piled high with fresh whipped cream and juicy strawberries. I'm ashamed to admit it, but I ate nearly the whole thing by myself. With my bare hands, no less.

Moments later, Scott instructed me to wipe the bits of berries and cream off my face, then asked me to dance a couple of impromptu waltzes and a schottische with him— right there on the street. After all, we'd just seen ol' Bones take off with his sweetheart and twirl her around to a western swing. We couldn't let the old folks beat us completely into the ground. Scott and I were getting more childlike and frisky by the minute. Being around happy, unrestrained people over the age of 60 was beginning to have a youthful effect on us.

As the sun began to fade and the autumn air cooled, we found ourselves wandering back in the direction of our "Irish" friend. As we'd hoped, Ray was still happily "sawing" away. The crowds were gone, so Scott and I sat down, propped our feet up on empty chairs, and listened to the music serenade the nightfall. A younger man on Ray's left was doing a fine job of picking his banjo, a woman to his right was belting out an old mournful ballad as she strummed her guitar. After a couple of melancholy tunes, Ray looked up at us and winked.

"These old songs are so sad, it's a wonder we're not all depressed."

I laughed and said, "It's okay. Just sing us a 'hallelujah' song in between the depressin' ones now and then."

"I'd like to do you one better than that, right after we finish this next heartbreaker."

Scott put his arm around me and stroked my shoulder as we waited, peacefully, for our love-graced day to come gently to its end. The group sang its last sad song for my husband and me, their only audience. No matter. These artists performed for the simple pleasure of sending their music into the air. Finally, the young banjo player set his instrument down, looked at the woman, at Ray, at us.

"Now this has been what I call a festival!" he declared.

Scott and I rose to give the group a two-person standing ovation, but Ray asked us to sit for just a minute longer.

"I'd like to say an Irish blessing for you two."

With that, he stood, swept the derby from his head and placed it over his heart once more, pronouncing a benediction befitting the day.

> *May the road rise up to meet you...may the sun shine warm upon your face...the rains fall soft upon your fields...and until we meet again, may God hold you in the palm of His hand.*

We walked away from that crisp fall evening, feeling somehow younger, almost reborn, for having been in the presence of benevolent elders who had learned the fine art of staying childlike at heart.

They will still bear fruit in old age, they will stay fresh and green.

PSALM 92:14

Winter is on my head, but eternal spring is in my heart.
Victor Hugo

19

Can I Hug the Bunny?

Finding Comfort in Fluff

I picked up Paula Payne Hardin's book *What Are You Going to Do with the Rest of Your Life?* and settled into my overstuffed rocker for a reading respite between daily duties. My eyes fell on a chapter entitled "The Child of Yesterday, The Adult of Today" and found my heart warmed by her personal, childlike confession.

"One day I realized I wanted to go to a toy store and find a teddy bear," Paula shared. "This may appear foolish to some—a woman in her fifties wanting a teddy bear, but it was my desire. I found a wonderful furry creature who called out to me from his deep-set brown eyes. I was so excited!" She even wrote a sonnet of her experience called "In Praise of Teddy Bears." In the sonnet she expresses how her bear comforted her with its soft, accepting presence. "So grownups, hug your bears with heart's delight!" the sonnet encourages.

"Come on," I'm sure some callused soul out there is protesting, "we're talkin' about a stuffed piece of fluff!" My child-heart answer to this logical argument is, "Never underestimate the power of fluff!"

Even my upper-level business executive father still keeps his old, pitiful, adorable, gray stuffed elephant in the top of his closet. The fur has mostly been rubbed off, and one of its button eyes is—sorry to say this, Daddy—nothing but a socket of stuffing. But don't make fun of this stuffed baby elephant around my father. He transforms instantly into a boy of about five. "That was my Dumbo," he softly reminisces, and I can almost visualize my daddy as a little boy going off to sleep with his arms around his baby elephant.

On my trip to Disneyland I bought a brand-new, stuffed Dumbo and mailed it off to my father. I wasn't back home in Texas for long before my parents showed up for a visit. When I opened the front door, there stood my Dad, stroking the velvet pink ears of his new baby elephant toy. In his classic "little boy" voice he said, "I like my Dumbo." Mother shook her head in mock worry.

"Becky" she said, "he's been under so much stress at work lately, I'm a little worried he's going to take that elephant into a board meeting."

When Scott was young, he had a stuffed monkey. He also had an imaginary friend named Joe, who lived in the closet. When Scott talks of Joe and his monkey, his voice slides back in time until he's sounding like a small boy. Funny how people do that. Everyone I ask about their special childhood companion begins to revert, without thinking, to using baby talk as they describe their treasured friends.

As an adult, my husband continues to keep friendly stuffed animals around. But now, he has a more macho name for his collection. They are, you see, his "truck mascots." He has a soft, squishy cow with long spindly legs. Ingeniously, he named her "Cow." Recently he added a stuffed moose to the front-seat menagerie. You guessed it: "Moose."

My children have also had their assorted stuffed "friends." Zach took lots of teasing over it, but when he was a little tyke he toted around "Buddy"—a stuffed boy dressed in overalls and a cap. Zeke had a fluff-and-battery-filled Glo-Worm that lit up the dark night. He dubbed it his "Glo-Buggy," though his father and I secretly called it his Bed Bug. Rachel, at age 12, was completely enamored with her stuffed Pooh Bear. She even had a Winnie-the-Pooh birthday party in her late teens. At the time of this writing, toddler toys are "in" with teens right now. Have you noticed? In the malls more and more teenagers are sporting Piglet watches, Mickey Mouse shirts, and Tweety Bird ball caps. They beat satanic rock group attire all to pieces.

Gabe, now 15, owns Big Bear—a huge, floppy, huggable bear three feet tall and three feet wide. Even when Gabe was only three feet tall himself, he'd insist on taking Big Bear everywhere. (I even let him take Big Bear to the grocery store with us. *Where*, I now wonder, *did I ever put the groceries?* Desperate moms will find a way to put up with anything if it keeps their preschoolers quiet on shopping trips.) Seven years later, Big Bear still occupies one fourth of Gabe's bed. He says he still loves his bear and "will never, ever get rid of him."

As my sweet grandmother, Nonnie, moved into her 80s, someone gave her a pretty, soft doll with flaxen hair and a pink folk-style dress. Nonnie named the doll Ursula and kept her primped and propped on her bed. Grandchildren and great-grandchildren could freely play with anything in Nonnie's house, but it always made her nervous if little grubby fingers got too close to her Ursula.

One day Nonnie had a stroke and had to enter the cold starkness of a hospital. Ursula came along, too. I remember Mother commenting on how bittersweet it was to see her aging mother comforted, in strange antiseptic surroundings, by the presence of a familiar doll.

As I thought about the teddy bear sonnet, and the stuffed animals that had comforted my family members, I felt a bit sad—as though I'd missed out on something wondrous and only now realized it. I never embraced, with my heart, one special stuffed piece of lovable fluff as a child. I had a doll that I loved, but no soft bear or monkey or elephant that I called my own and carried with me everywhere. So I closed the book, rose from my chair, grabbed my car keys, and headed to the toy store on a personal mission. It happened to be in the spring of the year, near Easter. Adorable bunnies of every conceivable style, shape, and color beckoned from store shelves to my child-heart, seeming to call out "Take me home! Pick me!" I finally settled on squishy, soft-furred rabbit with enormous floppy ears and oversized feet adorned with red calico pads. He fit perfectly in my arms.

And so this is how, at age 37, I found myself marching up to a toy store counter to buy my very own bunny. I took him home and placed him right on my pillow. I absolutely *love* him. This whole fluffy affair has turned into something of a sweet family joke. When the kids are sick or need some TLC, they'll pitifully moan, "Mom, can I borrow your bunny?"

Scott came home once after an especially grueling day at the office, stretched out on the couch, and stared blankly at the ceiling. When I asked him what I could do to help, he gruffly replied, "Bring me that old bunny."

This very afternoon I met a precious woman who often hosts women's retreats in her log home. She also collects teddy bears. As we intermittently talked and sipped hot orange-cinnamon tea from porcelain mugs, Suzie said, "One time I was preparing for the ladies to come, and I felt the Lord wanted me to give away three of my bears. So I set them aside, thinking to myself, *Oh, they are going to think this is so silly.* But during a sharing time, three of the woman told heartbreaking stories of childhood abuse. Then I told them what God had impressed upon me earlier and handed each woman a bear saying, 'God wants you to enjoy a second turn at childhood, starting *now.*' The women couldn't say anything. They just hugged those bears and bawled. It was beautiful."

Every grown-up who has ever been a child—or is part child still—understands that there is more to bunnies and bears and monkeys than fluff and stuff.

In a popular story about a little boy who was afraid of the dark, the mother tells her son that he can rest assured that God is always with him, even in the night.

"Yes," the little boy answers, "but I need somebody with skin on."

In the absence of "somebody with skin on," in the absence of a nice, soft person covered with skin, I believe the next best thing to snuggle up with in the dark is something soft and fluffy with fur on.

No matter how old you are, if you don't have a bear or a bunny or a cow or a moose, I encourage you to close this book, grab your keys, and head to the toy store to see which piece of fluff seems to be calling your name. You'll soon find yourself holding a soft, precious bit of childhood again—right in your very own grownup-kid-hands.

The poor man had nothing except one little ewe lamb he had bought.... It grew up with him and his children...and even slept in his arms....

2 Samuel 12:3

20

Let's Play Dress-Up!

A Unique Sense of Fashion

I've always believed in allowing people—including little people—the freedom to dress in ways that express their own personalities. Perhaps this explains why, years ago when my kids were small, one visiting youngster asked me if he could "wear his shirt inside out and backward like Zach and Zeke always do."

I've always worn originals. (At least people have always told me, "Becky, that outfit looks very, um, *original*.") This has not been easy for my husband to accept because he cares—deeply—about blending in with society's norms when it comes to public attire. As one might guess by now, blending in with the crowd has never been a top priority with me.

When Scott and I were newlyweds, all of 18 and 19 years old (respectively), my husband insisted we always walk, rather than drive, to our classes at the college campus located about a mile from our home. On chilly winter mornings, dressing for warmth rather than for success was my goal. My priorities made Scott more than a little nervous. As I roved through the house, tossing layer after layer of whatever laundry was handy upon my shivering form, Scott would beg, "Becky...wait...*please...not* the wool socks on your hands!"

"We've been through this a hundred times," I'd reply, digging through his sock drawer. "My hands get numb when they're cold, and only your wool socks seem to keep them warm enough."

"Okay. Put footwear on your hands if you must, but that red bandanna you've been tying around the outside of your coat hood—*that* has to go!"

"Scott, I need to keep my hood tied in close to my ears or the wind gets in there and makes them hurt and pound."

"Parading down the street with my bride dressed like a walking garage sale makes *my heart* hurt and pound."

"Ever since I was a little girl, this is the way I've dressed— in layers—to keep warm. My parents always thought it was cute—sort of a ragamuffin effect. Anyway, I refuse to freeze my diastecrutus for the sake of fashion."

"Just tell me one thing," Scott said as he lowered himself wearily on the edge of our bed. "When do you suppose you will be growing out of this childhood phase? Listen, Becky, we all have to wave our goodbyes to Puff the Magic Dragon, put away our pirate costumes, and move on from Honah Lee." He stopped his lecture for a second, then scratched his head. "And what, pray tell, is a *diastecrutus?*"

"I have no idea. But my mother always warned us never to let it freeze." I raised one eyebrow in warning. "And who knows what evil might befall you if it does?"

And so the conversation would end. Usually, we'd compromise. I'd wear the socks and bandanna; Scott would walk a block in front of me, pretending not to know who I was. Little did I know that, years later, I'd get a small taste of what Scott must have been feeling when my last-born child insisted on dressing himself and parading the results in public. Unfortunately, I did not have the option of forcing my three-year-old to walk a block in front of me, so I could pretend I wasn't his mother.

My youngest child, as you may have already guessed, is—well, *different*. As soon as Gabriel was old enough to have a say in the matter, he refused to wear jeans and shirts like the other kids. Wearing them inside out and backward wasn't even an appealing option to him.

It started out innocently enough. First, he began wearing the standard Superman cape. Just a portable plastic cape adorned with an iron-on "S." No big deal—except for the fact that he wore it every walking and sleeping moment. And it didn't take long for Gabe to move on to greater things. Batman came next, and his Batman cape of choice turned out to be my black half-slip secured around his neck by a large, pink, diaper pin. (Wouldn't psychologists have a heyday analyzing that?) Eventually the sight of my personal lingerie on display about town stopped bothering me, though it continued to cause Gabe's older siblings great fits of public humiliation.

It is important to remember these costumes were worn constantly, everywhere that Gabe went, 24 hours a day, for weeks at a time. To ask Gabe to go out the door without his costume would be like someone requesting that you or I take a downtown stroll in nothing but our socks and underwear. Gabe's costumes *were* his identity, his preschool power clothes. Without them—horrors!—someone might mistake Gabe for a mild-mannered, average Clark Kent-type preschooler and not recognize him for the incredible, zowie-wowie superhero he knew himself to be.

In October, things really began to get out of hand. Even I, who've always been proud of the fact that I'm a free spirit when it comes to matters of dress (not to mention immune to most forms of embarrassment), began to grow self-conscious when I left the house with my son. This, too, began innocently enough.

Several weeks before Gabe's fourth birthday, he commenced begging for a real fireman's costume.

"And, Momma," Gabe insisted, "I don't want one of those Halloween sissy fireman suits. I want *real* fireman rubber boots and a *real* fireman coat and a *real* red fireman's hat. And, 'specially, I want a gas mask."

Silly me. I obliged. Oh boy, did I oblige. It was a cinch to find a tall pair of rubber boots. After much slicker-searching, I happened upon a bright yellow one—heavy-duty rubber with a hood. I even found a large plastic hatchet in a discount bin. The perfect red hat was ripe for the picking at a local toy store and, as an added bonus, it made a piercing siren noise when its button was pressed. (Within two hours, the siren's batteries mysteriously disappeared. Who in the world could have done that?)

But the coup de grace—a sheer stroke of creative genius—was the "gas mask," which was actually one of those bright orange pollen masks that allergy sufferers wear when they mow the lawn. (My husband, by the way, is an allergy sufferer. But being the fashion-conscious guy that he is, he would rather be buried alive in grass clippings and found unconscious from a sneezing overdose than chance being seen in public wearing one of those "nerd" masks.)

As you might imagine, the costume was a smashing success. For weeks that turned into months, Gabe wore the entire fireman ensemble—complete with gas mask—everywhere we went. Rain or shine. Cool weather or unseasonable heat wave. And Gabe took his fireman duties seriously and stood ready to douse a fire or rescue someone from a burning building at the slightest sound of a smoke alarm. (Since our smoke alarm doubles as our dinner bell, he had quite a bit of practice.) I even have a much-prized picture of Gabriel at the mall, sitting on Santa's knee, dressed in his full fire-fighting regalia. Poor Santa had trouble understanding what my son wanted for Christmas, since Gabe refused to talk to the jolly ol' elf without the mask secured firmly over his young mouth.

I don't remember what Santa actually gave Gabe for Christmas that year, but I do recall that my friend Mary gave Gabriel his best-loved present of the season. It was a polyester trench coat, so long it barely skimmed the top of Gabe's tennis shoes, and a matching hat in a brilliant shade of yellow. From that day until Easter, Gabriel was Dick Tracy. I was so grateful to see my son's mouth ungraced by orange plastic and disposable filters that I welcomed "Detective Gabe" with open arms.

Today, as a teenager, Gabe has, surprisingly, adopted his daddy's taste in clothing preferences. Very aware of what's "cool," he now chooses clothes that help him blend, with style, into the cool world of high school. The Superman cape, the fireman suit, and the yellow trench coat have all gone the way of magic dragons, "sealing wax, and other fancy stuff."

"And what about Gabe's mother?" you ask. "Did she ever leave her childish ways behind and acquire some fashion sense?"

Well, it's like this. I'm about to go out for a walk. It's a cold and rainy day out there, so I'll need my hooded coat. And, of course, a pair of wool socks for my hands and a red bandanna to secure the hood so my ears won't hurt and pound.

My husband? These days, he's proud to take long, meandering walks with me—no matter what I'm wearing. All he asks is that I give him a 45-second lead before I begin my "frolic in the autumn mist"—preferably, a good 20 paces behind him.

Your beauty should not come from outward adornment....Instead, it should be that of your inner self.

1 Peter 3:3-4

21

Will You Tuck Me In?

Taking Comfort in Bedtime Rituals

Nighty-night, sleep tight, and don't let the bedbugs bite."

How many of us were tucked into bed and left with this parental sign-off ringing in our ears as we lay in the darkness? Interpreted literally this night-night farewell says, "Sweet dreams my little one—and by the way, I'd keep a sharp eye out for biting insects crawling under the covers if I were you."

Many of American nighttime routines—from childhood to adulthood—are totally lacking in logic. Nonetheless, we all find comfort in our family bedtime rituals, no matter how unusual. I have several of my own "goodnight, sweet dreams" traditions. Almost every night, I grab a good book or magazine and head to my tub full of hot-as-I-can-stand-it water. When I've steamed and read long enough that my eyes refuse to decode another word and my toes have turned to ten wrinkly prunes, I know I'm preheated and ready for bed. Once snuggled under the covers, I spoon into the curve of my sleeping husband and drop contentedly off to sleep. (Unless my sleeping husband is just pretending and not actually ready for full-fledged sleep. But I...um... digress.)

As far back as I can remember, a hot bath, a good book, and snuggling up (with a pillow or blankie in the days before Scott was handy), have been part of my nightly routine. On the other hand, Scott has his own method of going off to dreamland. As soon as he realizes it's a proper time to retire, he stumbles toward the bedroom, peeling off excess garments as he goes. *While* he is actually plummeting toward the bed, he falls asleep—midair—*before* his head hits the pillow. It never ceases to amaze me.

Most often Scott and I have our pillow talk before *he* goes to bed—for obvious reasons. Unless I'm simply in the mood to hear myself chattering a soliloquy, I have to catch my husband before he begins that unconscious descent toward his pillow. As one might imagine, our diverse bedtime routines have also been the cause of some ongoing conflict. Not long ago, after a rough night's sleep, we tried to discuss our sleeping preferences rationally. I opened the debate.

● ● ●

"Scott, I understand that you like to have some fresh air coming in the room. All I'm asking is that it not be of the

Arctic variety. I keep expecting snow flurries to come through the air vents at any moment."

"Becky," Scott calmly replied, "just because your feet never thaw does not mean the rest of us like to sleep with the temperature set on broil. What you need to do is tuck your head under the covers, like me, and you'll be warm as toast."

"I can't! It makes me claustrophobic. Look, I'm gasping for air just thinking about it."

Scott rolled his eyes toward the ceiling. "Do you think you could possibly be a little more dramatic?"

I pressed on, ignoring him. "Hey, O Toasty One, you wouldn't even let me warm my feet on your calves last night! What's up with that?"

"You kept pinching my leg hairs with your toenails. It's like Chinese torture."

"Okay, well, while we're on the subject of bedtime problems, I want to know why you and the kids go so ballistic whenever a teensy, weensy shred of light slithers its way into your rooms?'

"Shred of light? *Shred of light?* Beck, you are leaving the kitchen, hall, and bathroom lights on every night. The only thing we're lacking is a rotating searchlight in each closet!"

I clucked my tongue. "Now look who's being dramatic. Listen, I need lights on in the house so I can see my way to the children should they need me in case of a fire. Or a burglar. Or a stomach virus."

"That's ridiculous."

"Yeah, well obviously you've never groped in the darkness for a nauseous kid. Believe me, it only takes once."

● ● ●

There is no end in sight to these debates. Amazingly, I keep loving Scott in spite of his weird habits. (It's so nice to be the one in charge of the slant this book takes.) Somehow we've managed to get in at least a few hours of sleep each night for the past 25 years.

Speaking of sleep, I recall, with great fondness the way our two oldest boys used to wind down for bed as teenagers—and even now when Zach and Zeke are out of the house and on their own!

One night I was typing on the computer and Zeke was in an easy chair beside me, silently reading his homework assignment. Zachary, the oldest, opened the door to "check and see if Zeke was ready for bed yet." The boys always shared a room (they had no choice), and their bedtime routine consisted of listening to music, discussing stuff they think adults are too old to understand, and arguing about whose turn it is to turn off the light.

Zachary looked so forlorn peeking his head around the door, dressed in his boxer shorts and baggy T-shirt, that I couldn't resist teasing him a bit.

"Poor Zachary," I said in my syrupy-mommy voice, "can't you get off to sleep without your little brother and your nighty-night pillow talk?"

Zach stifled a sheepish grin while unconvincingly denying my charge. Then he checked on Zeke once more, not five minutes later, to see if he was "done yet." Despite Zach's protests, it was obvious to all of us that he enjoyed his evening chats with his brother.

When the children were young, we had elaborate bedtime routines always ending with Scott or me tucking them into bed after a little chat. Somewhere, over the years, our children all turned into teenagers, and our nighty-night roles reversed. Our teens began dropping by *our* bed for pillow talk, propping themselves onto the edges and the end of our mattress, one by one, as they wandered in late from dates, football games, or college classes. By the time they'd all arrived home, our bed looked like a scene from a wacky sitcom. Do you remember the old game of seeing how many people can fit into a phone booth? At our house it is "how many teenagers can sit on one queen-sized mattress" tucked in around their sleep-deprived parents. (I still don't understand why I can barely get a teen to grunt "hi" when *I'm* wide awake and ready for conversation, but when I am nearly unconscious with drowsiness, way beyond being able to engage in comprehendible chitchat, my kids suddenly turn into teenaged Oprahs and Larry Kings.)

Not only do our own kids show up for late-night chats around the "family bed," but often they invite their friends to the foot of our bed the way others invite their friends to relax at the kitchen table. "Pull up a piece of mattress and sit down," they'll say casually.

This past Thanksgiving evening we had, in and around our bed, all four of our kids, along with Zeke's wife Amy, Rachel's fiancé Jody, our Brittany Spaniel Daisy, and Zeke and Amy's puppy Whispers (our "granddog"). All we needed was a "piggy we stole from the shed," and we could have been the folks from John Denver's "Grandma's Feather Bed."

Sure, Scott and I tease and hem and haw about the noisy, crowded scene on our bedspread that has turned into a Freeman family tradition. But the truth is, we wouldn't trade having a gaggle of growing kids tuck us into bed for all the feathers in our sagging mattress.

Well, it's about that time again. The clock is about to strike 10:00, and I've spent my pillow-talk moments with you, my reader friend. So to all a good night. Please do sleep tight. And even though I think it might be psychologically destructive to say this—don't let the bedbugs bite.

I will lie down and sleep in peace, for you alone, O LORD, make me dwell in safety.

PSALM 4:8

22

Daddy, I Can Fly!

Delighting Abba

Although I love the slinky, silky gowns my husband gives me every holiday season, this year I asked if he might give me something a little less breezy. I was particularly interested in sleepwear that would wrap warm and snugly around my cold, cold feet.

Thinking it would be a cute joke, Scott gave me a pair of woman-sized pink-and-white feety pajamas in a teddy bear print. Christmas evening, I stole away to the bedroom and tried them on just for fun. As I put one foot and then another into the pajama legs I drifted back to the very first memory I have as a child. I could almost hear my Daddy, as he sounded nearly 35 years ago, softly singing, "Put your little foot, put your little foot, put your little foot right here" as I stood on my bed while he helped me into my feety PJs.

● ● ●

My father is one man who has managed, all his life, to keep his child-heart pumping strong. One rainy, spring afternoon when I was about 11, I went into the garage and found my father ascending a ladder into the attic. Though Daddy was sentimental, he was *not* a handyman, so the sight of a ladder provoked my curiosity. Then he crooked his finger in a silent gesture that I knew meant "Come along, but be quiet."

I followed him up into the attic and sat down beside him, curious as to the nature of our exploration. But all my dad said was, *"Shhh...listen."* Then I heard it. The rain, pattering overhead, being amplified by our nearness to the rooftop.

"I come up here whenever it rains," Daddy said softly. It was cool and comforting, a tender moment caught like a snapshot in my mind.

● ● ●

To my pleasant surprise, my husband turned out to be a rain-on-the-roof kind of guy, too. He even built our bed so that the head of it fits snugly against a large picture window. At night, if the full moon is shining or a soft rain is falling, Scott pulls up the blinds and raises the window and whispers, *"Shhh...Becky. Listen."* And this, I believe, is part of the reason why the two men I love most in the whole world are my daddy and my husband.

● ● ●

Another thing I loved about Daddy was the way he gave us kids silly nicknames. My little sister, Rachel, he nicknamed

"The Bunky." Or sometimes he called her "Yupupuh." (Don't ask me where he got the inspiration for these.) When my brother, David, was small, his word for "horses" came out as "saucies." Thus he earned the nickname "Saucy." When I was small, I wore a red ruffly nightgown, which I adored, and whenever I wore it Daddy called me his "Red Arriba." All of us kids collectively were dubbed "sproogins."

Another amazing thing about Daddy—in all my years I cannot ever recall him criticizing me. Not once. Always he would praise and encourage my efforts—however crazy, however childish they were.

● ● ●

Not long ago I had a dream—it's a reoccurring dream I've had for years. In it I can fly. I love these dreams, and while I'm in them I can't understand why other people don't float themselves up to the sky and join me. It is so easy, nothing to it! Most of the time I just spread out my arms and take off, but in one of my dreams I piloted a Frisbee. Now *that* was fun!

But this last dream I had was especially realistic. Once again I was flying and in my dream I thought to myself, *This is ridiculous. Nobody else is flying except me. I need to find out if this is real or if this is just my imagination.*

So I flew to my parents' home, knocked on the door, and floated up to the ceiling inside the house. Then I hovered over my father, who was looking at me, not at all surprised to find me up there. I said, "Daddy, listen. You've *got* to tell me the truth. I really think I'm flying. It feels so real, but I'm worried that this might just all be a dream."

My daddy's answer was swift and sure. "Honey," he said, "it's no dream. You're flying all right."

When I woke up I laughed, but then tears welled in my eyes. *How marvelous,* I thought, *even in my subconscious, in spite of all logic to the contrary, my father believes in me.*

For Father's Day last year, I could not find a card that seemed to fit how I felt about Daddy. Finally I came across the perfect one, though it was not in the Father's Day section. On the front there was a picture of Piglet walking side by side with Pooh toward a setting sun. Underneath the serene scene was their conversation.

> "Pooh?"
> "Yes, Piglet?"
> "I just wanted to make sure of you."

My dad has been like Pooh to me, his Piglet. Oh, we don't chitchat a whole lot, not like my mother and me anyway. But in every memory involving my father, from the time he sang, "Put your little foot" as he helped me into my feety pajamas to this latest dream where he assured me that yes, I could really fly, my father has been there in the shadows, cheering me on, giving me the steadfast assurance that always and forever I can be sure of him.

And so it is, Piglet-children everywhere, with our Father in heaven.

(My father, after reading this chapter, brought me a tiny-framed picture of Pooh writing on a long sheet of paper with a fancy pen, all the way from England. Enclosed was a note that said, "My Dear Piglet: Just wanted to be sure that you know I'll always be there and that it's fun to watch you fly. Love, Daddy.")

This resurrection life...[is] adventurously expectant, greeting God with a childlike "What's next, Papa?" God's Spirit touches our spirits and confirms who we really are...With God on our side like this, how can we lose?

ROMANS 8:14-17,31 THE MESSAGE

Growing Up to Be a Child

Mud-puddle miracles
Doodle-bug designs
Bursts of fun with bubblegum
Oh, to see life as a child!
"I love yous" big as rainbows
"I'm sorrys" from the heart
A kiss goodnight, a bearhug tight
To love as would a child!
"Let the children come to Me,"
He said with arms flung wide
Don't stop me now—
I'm coming, too
For I'm a child inside

I want to laugh from the belly
Risk playing a clown—
I'm giving up on growing up
From here on out I'm growing

D

O

W

N

Oh, Yeeeaahh.*

* Becky Freeman © 1997

Any of you who welcomes a little child like this because you are mine, is welcoming me and caring for me.

MATTHEW 18:5 TLB

Other Books by Becky

Chocolate Chili Pepper Love
Coffee Cup Friendship & Cheesecake Fun
Lemonade Laughter & Laid-Back Joy
Peanut Butter Kisses & Mud Pie Hugs
Real Magnolias
Worms in My Tea

For Kids

Camp Wanna Banana Mysteries
Gabe & Critters Series

Drop by for a visit at Becky's virtual "porch swing"
www.beckyfreeman.com
While there check out the Becky Bags!